The United States and Egypt

The United States and Egypt

An Essay on Policy for the 1990s

WILLIAM B. QUANDT

THE BROOKINGS INSTITUTION
Washington, D.C.

Copyright © 1990 by
THE BROOKINGS INSTITUTION
1775 Massachusetts Avenue, N.W., Washington, D.C. 20036

Library of Congress Cataloging-in-Publication data:

Quandt, William B.
  The United States and Egypt: an essay on policy for the 1990s /
William B. Quandt.
    p. cm.
  Includes bibliographical references.
  ISBN 0-8157-7295-5 (alk. paper)
  1. United States—Foreign relations—Egypt. 2. Egypt—Foreign re-
lations—United States. I. Title.
E183.8.E35Q36   1990
327.73062—dc20   90–34763
                                                              CIP

9 8 7 6 5 4 3 2 1

Typeset in Linotron Meridien
  by Graphic Composition, Inc.
    Athens, Georgia
Book design by Ken Sabol
Cover design by Hubert Leckie

THE BROOKINGS INSTITUTION

The Brookings Institution is an independent organization devoted to nonpartisan research, education, and publication in economics, government, foreign policy, and the social sciences generally. Its principal purposes are to aid in the development of sound public policies and to promote public understanding of issues of national importance.

The Institution was founded on December 8, 1927, to merge the activities of the Institute for Government Research, founded in 1916, the Institute of Economics, founded in 1922, and the Robert Brookings Graduate School of Economics and Government, founded in 1924.

The Board of Trustees is responsible for the general administration of the Institution, while the immediate direction of the policies, program, and staff is vested in the President, assisted by an advisory committee of the officers and staff. The by-laws of the Institution state: "It is the function of the Trustees to make possible the conduct of scientific research, and publication, under the most favorable conditions, and to safeguard the independence of the research staff in the pursuit of their studies and in the publication of the results of such studies. It is not a part of their function to determine, control, or influence the conduct of particular investigations or the conclusions reached."

The President bears final responsibility for the decision to publish a manuscript as a Brookings book. In reaching his judgment on the competence, accuracy, and objectivity of each study, the President is advised by the director of the appropriate research program and weighs the views of a panel of expert outside readers who report to him in confidence on the quality of the work. Publication of a work signifies that it is deemed a competent treatment worthy of public consideration but does not imply endorsement of conclusions or recommendations.

The Institution maintains its position of neutrality on issues of public policy in order to safeguard the intellectual freedom of the staff. Hence interpretations or conclusions in Brookings publications should be understood to be solely those of the authors and should not be attributed to the Institution, to its trustees, officers, or other staff members, or to the organizations that support its research.

Foreword

By most measures the U.S.-Egyptian relationship of the past fifteen years has been a success story. The two countries cooperated in negotiations that led to the historic Egyptian-Israeli peace treaty of 1979. The United States has provided substantial quantities of economic and military assistance to Egypt and has seen Egypt play a moderating role in the region.

With the waning of the cold war and the debate in the United States over foreign policy priorities and aid commitments, the time seems ripe for a look at the underpinnings of the U.S-Egyptian relationship. William B. Quandt, a senior fellow in the Brookings Foreign Policy Studies program, has been concerned with U.S.-Egyptian affairs, both as a scholar and as a government official, for more than twenty years. In this essay he assesses the strengths and weaknesses of the relationship and puts forward several ideas for strengthening the foundations for the 1990s. Most important, he proposes that the United States act to reduce Egypt's indebtedness and restructure the assistance program. He also places special emphasis on the importance of continuing to work with Egypt in promoting the Arab-Israeli peace process.

The author is grateful to many people for help in the course of this study. In particular, he would like to thank Ismat Abd al-Maguid, Muhammad Abdallah, Abd al-Munim Said Aly, Nabil al-Araby, Alfred L. Atherton, Usamah al-Baz, Boutros Boutros Ghali, Ali Hillal al-Din Dessouki, Hermann F. Eilts, Ashraf Ghorbal, Muhammed Hassanein Heikel, Saad ad-Din Ibrahim, Muhammad Ibrahim Kamil, Mustafa Khalil, Melinda Kimble, Ahmed Maher, Amre Moussa, Abd al-Rouf Reedy, Delwin Roy, Yahya Sadowski, Michael Van Dusen, Nicholas

Veliotes, Said Yassin, Frank Wisner, and Len Zuza. At Brookings, the author was assisted by Elisa Barsoum, Judy Buckelew, Susanne Lane, and Catherine Meehan. Caroline Lalire edited the manuscript; Amy R. Waychoff verified it; and Fred Kepler prepared the index.

Brookings gratefully acknowledges the financial support for this project provided by the John D. and Catherine T. MacArthur Foundation, the Rockefeller Foundation, and Ezra K. Zilkha.

The views expressed here are those of the author and should not be ascribed to any of the persons or organizations acknowledged above or to the officers, trustees, or other staff members of the Brookings Institution.

BRUCE K. MAC LAURY
President

March 1990
Washington. D.C.

Contents

The United States and Egypt

Introduction

The decade of the 1980s saw an unprecedented flow of diplomatic, economic, and military resources from the United
States to Egypt. During this period the U.S. Congress appropriated more than $23 billion in various forms of aid for Egypt.
Few foreign leaders were more highly regarded in official
circles in Washington than the Egyptian president. And the
two countries were often portrayed as particularly close friends
and allies.

The key to this apparent success of U.S.-Egyptian relations
was the achievement of peace between Egypt and Israel and
the willingness of successive American presidents and Congress to support high levels of economic and military assistance
to Egypt. During the sometimes feverish cold war atmosphere
of the mid-1980s, Egypt was also able to benefit, in some
American circles, from the perception that it was a "strategic
asset" in the struggle against Soviet influence.

As we look ahead to the next decade, it seems inevitable that
the underpinnings of U.S.-Egyptian relations will change. The
Arab-Israeli "peace process" may not provide much sustenance for either Cairo or Washington; the fading of the cold
war atmosphere will invalidate much of the strategic-asset argument; and the net impact of American aid is likely to go
down as debt repayments to the United States increase. All in
all, the 1990s may well see a shift from the primacy of political
and strategic issues to the dominance of economic concerns in
the U.S.-Egyptian dialogue. Unless managed with skill and determination, and with continuing sensitivity to political realities, economic problems could undermine the foundations of a
relationship that has served American interests well in recent
years.

1

One need not look back very far to be reminded of how unusual it is for Cairo and Washington to be on good terms. From the mid-1950s through the early 1970s, against a backdrop of regional instability and intense crises, the United States and Egypt typically found themselves at odds. The Arab-Israeli wars of 1967 and 1973 saw the United States essentially backing Israel against Egypt.

Then, in one of the great reversals of alignment in recent memory, Egypt began to move away from the Soviet Union and into the American orbit. By 1979 the United States had helped to engineer a peace treaty between Egypt and Israel. In the subsequent decade Egypt became the second largest recipient of American economic and military assistance—next to Israel. This change placed Egypt well ahead of such long-standing American allies in the third world as Turkey, Pakistan, and the Philippines in its claim on American resources.

Few Americans would question whether their national interests have been well served by this development. Aid to Egypt is widely seen as an integral part of Egyptian-Israeli peace, which is strongly supported by Congress and the American public. Although foreign aid is generally unpopular, Congress to date has only occasionally raised questions about the outlay of some $5 billion a year in commitments to Egypt and Israel, more than $2 billion of which goes to Egypt, largely as grant assistance.[1]

One might conclude from this brief description that U.S.-Egyptian relations represent a great success story in American foreign policy. To some extent such a judgment is justified, but with certain qualifications.

First, the United States and Egypt have not become, nor are they destined to be, full-fledged allies, despite the heavy flow

1. For a recent proposal to reduce aid to Egypt and Israel, see Senator Bob Dole, "To Help New Democracies, Cut Aid to Israel, 4 Others," *New York Times*, January 16, 1990, p. A27.

of American aid. The two countries still disagree on many issues, which has put some strain on their relationship. Even though Egypt and the United States forged their partnership in the Arab-Israeli peace process, this issue still can account for dissonance between Cairo and Washington.

Second, the underpinnings of the relationship are not particularly strong. Nothing in the U.S.-Egyptian relationship compares with the network of ties that links the United States to countries like Great Britain and Israel. The relationship has been developed at the level of governing elites, and it is still supported there, but the mass of Egyptians and Americans have few dealings with one another. In brief, a change of policy at the top could quickly alter the ties between the two countries, even though there would still be constraints working in both capitals against fundamental changes in the relationship.

Third, the relationship has already passed through its honeymoon period and is now beset by a range of problems, none of which seems fatal but each of which needs attention. Indicative of this change is the fact that when leaders of the two countries now meet, they are likely to dwell on problems of debt and economic reform as well as on the more edifying issues of Middle East peacemaking.

Fourth, recent history suggests that Egypt is uncomfortable with being dependent on powerful outsiders. The British presence in Egypt provoked a strong nationalist reaction in the 1930s and 1940s, as did the Soviet presence in the 1960s and 1970s. Not surprisingly, many Egyptian nationalists, as well as followers of the Islamist movements, are now outspokenly anti-American or at least critical of important aspects of American foreign policy.

Fifth, the dramatic changes taking place in central Europe and in U.S.-Soviet relations are likely to reduce the strategic importance of the Middle East for both superpowers. Washington might call for a reassessment not only of the traditional

3

props of U.S. diplomacy in the region—namely, economic and military aid—but also of its active involvement in the Arab-Israeli peace process. Significant American retrenchment on either or both of these fronts would immediately affect U.S.-Egyptian relations.

As Washington and Cairo look ahead to the management of their relationship in the 1990s, it is important to assess the strengths and weaknesses of the ties that bind them, to think of how best the relationship might evolve, and to try to establish a firmer, even if less intimate, basis for cooperation between two countries whose interests overlap but are not identical. First, however, it is necessary to analyze some of the structural realities of the relationship.

The Structure of U.S.-Egyptian Relations

Try as they might, leaders in Cairo and Washington are unable to ignore two fundamental aspects of their relations. The first is the enormous disparity in power between the two, a fact that makes a relationship of real equality almost impossible—a familiar problem in American dealings with all third world countries. The second aspect, however, is unique to U.S.-Egyptian relations. In short, Israel is an intrinsic part of the relationship. Bilateral ties between the United States and Egypt should really be seen as one side of a triangle, the other sides of which link the United States to Israel and Israel to Egypt. Any significant development in one part of the triangle can affect the other parts. In particular, any deterioration in Egyptian-Israeli relations will influence the ties between Washington and Cairo. Egyptians inevitably resent the fact that their country is valued less for its own importance than as a peace partner for Israel.[2]

The issue of power disparity is difficult for third world countries to handle in their relations with the former colonial powers of Europe, and even more so with the superpowers. Recognizing the problem, many newly independent countries rallied to the banner of "nonalignment." In practice, this slogan could mean several things: keeping a distance from both major powers; playing off one big power against another by flirting with both; or tilting toward one, but keeping the door open to the other. Real nonalignment, however, has been difficult to achieve, especially for countries that have regional am-

2. See Hermann Frederick Eilts, "The United States and Egypt," in William B. Quandt, ed., *The Middle East: Ten Years after Camp David* (Brookings, 1988), pp. 113–27.

bitions (and therefore want lots of arms), or that face crushing economic problems and think the way out is to win support from a rich patron.

Egypt, needless to say, is a country with both broad regional ambitions and severe economic difficulties. Thus the need for outside support is especially great, but so is the resentment when its freedom to maneuver is constrained by strings tied to aid. With a population above 50 million, and a recent history as the undisputed leader of the Arab world, Egypt cannot be classified as just one more poor, dependent third world country. Both the United States and the Soviet Union have learned that Egyptians are extremely proud of their country, very nationalistic, and suspicious that foreigners offering help are doing so for non-Egyptian reasons. Because of these special circumstances, Cairo's relations with powerful outsiders will always be somewhat problematic. Independence is a cherished ideal and a pillar of any Egyptian regime's legitimacy, but once Egypt turns to a major power for arms and economic assistance, it begins to slip away from nonalignment. Some price is always paid to the benefactor. At best, a country like Egypt can aspire to be a junior partner—a more polite term than client—but it cannot realistically expect to become a full-fledged ally. Nor do most Egyptians really want to see their country allied with any of the major world powers.

The power imbalance between Egypt and its benefactors, combined with the special sensitivities of Egyptians, creates conditions in which both parties to the relationship experience frustration. A weak country that becomes dependent on a superpower for arms and money is likely to become resentful rather than grateful. Real equality is unachievable, and it is hard to sell oneself as a strategic asset, especially if military bases and formal alliances are unacceptable to one's own public. The result is an uneasy relationship of dependence, a fear of exploitation, of co-optation, and of loss of control over one's destiny. For a time this situation can be justified by necessity—

6

a need for arms, money, or technical assistance—but the relationship is understandably troubled.

During periods of intense rivalry between the superpowers, small states have been able to exploit the competition to their own advantage. By threatening to switch partners, a dependent country may ensure considerate treatment from its patron. Although this threat cannot be used often, it is inherent in such a relationship and has been easily understood by both superpowers. Cold war competition between the superpowers, however, has made it difficult for a small state to avoid antagonizing one or the other. And enmity from either great power can be costly. Arms and aid may well start flowing to regional rivals, making it essential to the state to continue receiving support from either Moscow or Washington as a counterweight. In the past, polarization was the likely result, not nonalignment.[3]

One might assume that third world countries would find the costs of superpower rivalry excessive. But some leaders have learned to play the game well and have clearly benefited. An easing of superpower tensions, they fear, may make them less important on the global chessboard, or they may be sacrificed in the interest of agreements reached over their heads by the superpowers. Détente is not necessarily welcomed by regional powers with ambitions of their own. At worst, an easing of tensions between the superpowers may mean they will lose interest in supporting their traditional clients in the third world. And a loss of interest may mean a loss of aid and arms. Thus many in the Middle East are uneasy about the prospect of a post–cold war regional order.

From the perspective of the major power, winning over a new client is more satisfying than maintaining and subsidizing

3. The problem of polarization can be clearly seen as early as 1955, when the Western powers tried to organize some Arab states into an anti-Soviet alliance, while the Soviets sought to displace Western influence in Egypt by offering arms for sale.

one. Once a big power has achieved its basic goals—ousted its main rival, reduced the danger of uncontrolled conflict, gained access to facilities—it tends to take the new relationship for granted. Arms and aid may be routinely provided, but big powers have a hard time sustaining interest in the nuances of relations with small powers.

Whereas small powers are usually well attuned to political changes in Moscow or Washington, few American or Soviet leaders have the background or inclination to follow the twists and turns of policy in third world capitals. Some of their advisers may possess the required expertise to interpret events in the Middle East, but even that cannot be taken for granted.

Great powers are therefore notoriously insensitive to the local scene far from their borders. Patrons expect clients to be grateful and docile, which they rarely are for long. When difficulties arise, major powers expect clients to comply with their wishes and to play by their rules. Over time, they may begin to express frustration about the lack of gratitude for all the help they are giving. Public opinion in both countries can then become a problem.

If the issues stemming from the bonds of dependency are familiar, the role played by Israel in the Egyptian-American relationship is unique. Egypt alone among major recipients of American largesse must constantly worry about the ability of a third country to damage its ties to Washington. This reality is particularly galling to the Egyptian political elite, who believes the country was promised near equality of treatment with Israel by President Jimmy Carter. Indeed, during Carter's first meeting with Egyptian President Anwar Sadat in April 1977, Carter said, "I can see the possibility that ten years from now our ties to you in the economic, military, and political spheres will be just as strong as the ties we now have with Israel."[4]

Having held out this tempting vision, Carter immediately

4. Quoted in William B. Quandt, *Camp David: Peacemaking and Politics* (Brookings, 1986), p. 52.

added that it could be realized only if Egyptian-Israeli relations became strong. Sadat, who seemed to believe Egypt could match Israel as a strategic ally in the eyes of Washington, may not have appreciated the importance of Carter's qualification. (Had he been privy to the contents of any of Carter's many meetings with Israeli leaders, Sadat would have known that no comparable condition was ever mentioned in discussions of U.S.-Israeli relations.)

In practical terms the "Israeli factor" was not a great problem for Egypt when the peace process was moving forward. Egyptian and Israeli ties to Washington rose on the same wave. Trouble could start, however, if Egypt and Israel ever drifted apart. A foretaste of what might occur came in late 1982. After the Israeli invasion of Lebanon and the apparent Israeli complicity in the massacres by Lebanese forces of Palestinian civilians at Sabra and Shatila refugee camps in September, President Husni Mubarak withdrew Egypt's ambassador from Tel Aviv. He did not appoint a new ambassador until 1986. During this period members of Congress would regularly query the Egyptians on when they intended to return their ambassador to Tel Aviv. At times that seemed to be the most important issue in the bilateral relationship.

This episode (involving the return of the Egyptian ambassador to Tel Aviv) helped to remind the Egyptians that they lacked a vital ingredient in their relationship with Washington; namely, a strong domestic constituency in the United States. Israel's comparative advantage, in essence, derived from its influence on domestic American politics. Sadat had tried, with some success, to court American public opinion and to develop support for Egypt in Congress, but his assassination in October 1981 removed the basis for the special relationship. He had successfully sold himself, but not Egypt. His successor, Husni Mubarak, has neither the inclination nor the flare for public relations American-style.

Egyptians find it irritating that American support for their country is largely a function of Egypt's willingness to live in peace with Israel. For them, that is a flaw in the relationship. But, ironically, the Israeli connection is almost certainly a source of strength in the relationship as well. What other Arab country can be fairly confident of the acquiescence of the American pro-Israeli lobby when it comes to arms transfers? Countries such as Turkey and the Philippines, both of which are formal allies of the United States and provide military bases of strategic value, receive far less aid than Egypt. Without the Israeli connection, Egypt might well be viewed by Washington in much the same light as Pakistan—a strategically important country with interests that overlap with, but are not identical to, those of the United States. Pakistan, which has twice the population of Egypt and a smaller gross national product (GNP) per capita, receives about one-fourth as much economic and military assistance from the United States as Egypt does.[5]

Egypt is faced with a dilemma. It wants the economic and military assistance that Washington alone can provide, but it bridles at constraints on its independence, resents being treated as a client, and finds the intrusiveness of the Israeli factor in the relationship with Washington both insulting and domestically unpopular. Are these frustrations enough to bring its close ties with Washington to an end? Does the history of Soviet-Egyptian relations provide any clues about the future of the U.S.-Egyptian relationship?

5. It is estimated that in fiscal year 1989 the United States gave $350.30 million in economic aid to Pakistan and $230.92 in military aid, for a total of $581.22 million. The comparable figures for Turkey were $60.35 million, $503.40 million, and $563.75 million; and for the Philippines, $351.44 million, $127.60 million, and $479.04 million. U.S. Agency for International Development, *Congressional Presentation, Fiscal Year 1990: Main Volume*, p. 287.

Lessons from the Past

One of the most dramatic Soviet breakthroughs into the third world came in 1955 with the introduction of Soviet arms to Egypt, the so-called Czech arms deal. Twenty years later Soviet-Egyptian relations had collapsed. Moscow had little to show for its massive involvement in Egypt and could do nothing to prevent Egypt from moving into the American camp.

A closer examination of Soviet-Egyptian relations suggests that two distinct phases can be identified. During the first ten years the two countries were building an alliance. Arms aid was followed by economic assistance. By the early 1960s Egypt was beginning to model its own economy somewhat on Soviet lines. So close were relations between the two countries that by 1967 Soviet leaders felt they could ask Egypt's president, Gamal Abd al-Nasser, to mobilize his troops to try to ward off a possible Israeli threat to the regime in Syria. Nasser complied, perhaps realizing that by such a move he might restore his sagging regional fortunes and his battered personal prestige. The June 1967 war was the result.[6]

The second decade of Soviet-Egyptian relations was much more troubled than the first. As the price of its continuing support to the hard-pressed Egyptian regime, the Soviet Union asked for and received air and naval bases in Egypt. The Soviet military presence rose to at least 15,000 in the early 1970s, and during the so-called war of attrition in 1970, Soviet pilots flew combat sorties along the Suez Canal, losing four planes to Israeli fire in the process.

6. In the summer of 1988 a leading Soviet expert on the Middle East confirmed in an interview with the author that Moscow had encouraged Nasser to mobilize his armed forces in May 1967 in order to deter Israel from striking at Damascus.

By the time Nasser died in September 1970, Egypt was deeply dependent on the Soviet Union, and resentments were growing on both sides, but especially in Cairo. Nasser's successor, Anwar Sadat, was no favorite of the Soviets, and early in 1971 he faced a serious challenge from holdovers from Nasser's era who were believed to be close to Moscow. Whatever the truth behind the coup attempt in the spring of 1971, Sadat concluded that the Soviet Union had tried to engineer his ouster. And he may well have been correct.

Although Sadat was obliged to sign a friendship treaty with the Soviet Union as the price for continued support, by mid-1972 he was ready to move independently. With little advance notice, he asked the Soviets to withdraw the bulk of their military advisers in July 1972; almost immediately he secretly contacted the Nixon administration.[7]

Failing to find a way out of the impasse with Israel through diplomacy, Sadat took steps to ensure the regular flow of Soviet arms in late 1972, then decided on war in the spring of 1973. Despite his strained relations with Moscow, Sadat counted on continuing military support from the Soviets as well as their diplomatic backing. On October 6, 1973, Egypt and Syria launched a successful surprise attack against Israel, gaining momentary advantages and provoking a crisis of global size. Although the Soviet Union rushed to the aid of both Damascus and Cairo, it was to Washington that Sadat addressed his most urgent pleas for help as the war came to a close. Within weeks of the cease-fire, Secretary of State Henry A. Kissinger was in Cairo. Soviet-Egyptian relations never recovered during the Sadat era, as the United States moved quickly to monopolize the diplomatic arena.[8]

7. See Henry Kissinger, *White House Years* (Little, Brown, 1979), pp. 1292–1300; and William B. Quandt, *Decade of Decisions: American Policy toward the Arab-Israeli Conflict, 1967–1976* (University of California Press, 1977), pp. 152–59.
8. Quandt, *Decade of Decisions*, pp. 207–29.

For nearly ten years the Soviets had almost no presence, and even less influence, in Cairo. By 1985 relations had been normalized, but the special relationship of the 1960s remained only a fading memory. And Moscow's preoccupations with both internal affairs and the upheavals in central Europe seem sure to keep the Soviets from committing much in the way of time, energy, or resources to Egypt or elsewhere in the Middle East in the 1990s.

Some Egyptians profess to see similarities in the pattern of Egypt's relations with both Moscow and Washington. The early phase was one of euphoria, of high expectations, of shared interest as the new patron helped Egypt to pursue its interests. This period lasted for a few years before mundane issues of arms supply, economic aid, and debt repayment began to cause problems.

If one dates the onset of the current phase of U.S.-Egyptian relations to about 1972–73, then one might expect, based on the Soviet experience, for stress to start to show in the early 1980s. That period happens to coincide with Sadat's assassination, Mubarak's coming to power, the Israeli invasion of Lebanon, and Egypt's withdrawal from a major role in the Arab-Israeli peace process. By 1983–84 U.S.-Egyptian relations were indeed subject to strains, especially over problems of debt repayment and Egypt's perception of American bias in Israel's favor.

The model of Soviet-Egyptian relations, if taken seriously, would suggest that sometime in the early 1990s Egypt and the United States might come to a serious parting of the ways. But the dynamics of the two sets of relations are not likely to be identical. For one thing, the Soviets relied primarily on arms supplies to influence Egypt, though they probably never thought they could provide enough arms for Egypt to defeat Israel. Indeed, the Egyptian experience with Soviet arms in the wars of 1967 and 1973 did not lead to feelings of gratitude

13

toward the Soviets. In short, the Soviets were never able to deliver on the main issue that had led the Egyptians to ask them for help in the first place. A complete break with Moscow would remove the "war option" for Egypt for a long time, but in any event that option was no longer very viable after 1973.

In contrast to the way it approached the Soviet Union, Egypt turned to the United States primarily with political and economic objectives in mind. First, Sadat wanted urgent American help in the peace process. If possible, he wanted the United States to engineer a comprehensive Arab-Israeli peace. At a minimum, he wanted to recover Sinai for its appreciable assets (oil and the Suez Canal) and for its role as a buffer with Israel. This lesser objective the United States was able to achieve with the two disengagement agreements of 1974 and 1975 and the Camp David Accords in 1978. Egypt received nearly complete satisfaction on this score.

Second, Egypt hoped the United States would be able to provide economic assistance, technology, and investment to promote economic growth. A regime that could no longer ensure its legitimacy by mobilizing against the Israeli enemy or leading the Arab world could at least hope to win support by improving the lot of the people. Expectations outstripped performance in this area. During the 1980s many Egyptians began to question the value of the American connection, a sentiment particularly felt within Islamic political movements.

Still, any Egyptian government would have to consider two questions if it contemplated a break with Washington: first, who would restrain Israel from reconquering Sinai in some future crisis; and second, who would replace, and on what terms, the approximately $2.3 billion in economic and military aid Egypt receives each year from Washington? The Arab oil producers had money but would attach strings of their own that might be onerous. The Europeans had arms but would demand payment for them. The Soviets could do little to help the economy but might be a plausible source of some arms. In brief, there was no easy substitute for American support, although some combination of outside assistance might fill the gap. The alternative to Soviet help in 1973–74 was much easier to contemplate than the alternative to U.S. help in the late 1980s, and therefore the incentive for Egypt to switch patrons was greater in the earlier period.

This suggests that a sharp downturn in U.S.-Egyptian relations, following the pattern of Soviet-Egyptian dealings in the 1960s and early 1970s, is not inevitable. It is, however, possible. Choices exist on both sides concerning how to manage the relationship in the years ahead. It is unlikely that the honeymoon era could be recreated, but a goal of maintaining normal, correct relations that serve mutual interests seems attainable. Before turning to specific policy choices in Washington that might improve chances of reaching that goal, let us look in greater depth at the main elements of the current relationship between Cairo and Washington.

Politics and Diplomacy

As noted, the present American-Egyptian relationship is a product of the October 1973 war and its immediate aftermath. Sadat went to war with the objective of drawing the two superpowers into the diplomatic arena, hoping that they would then broker a settlement of the conflict with Israel. To fight the war, Sadat had needed Moscow. But to reach a settlement of the conflict, he needed Washington. Thus Sadat began to communicate directly with President Richard M. Nixon and Secretary of State Kissinger while the war was still going on. His message was clear: once the war was over, he wanted the United States to play the central role in peacemaking.

The American role in bringing the war to an end helped to forge the new relationship with Egypt. As the war was coming to an end, the two superpowers agreed on a cease-fire resolution, to go into effect on October 22, 1973. The Israelis ignored the stand-still provisions of the resolution and continued to advance in the hope of cutting off the Egyptian Third Army Corps, then entrapped on the east bank of the Suez Canal. Nixon and Kissinger did not want to see Sadat humiliated by the Israelis. Nor did they want the Soviets to intervene to save Sadat. They therefore fashioned a dual policy: declaring a stage-three nuclear alert as a warning to the Soviets and giving a sharp message to the Israelis not to continue their advance. As a result, the Americans emerged as the party that saved Sadat from a possible last-minute defeat. That, at least, is how the Americans perceived their role,[9] and Sadat, unlike most Egyptians, seemed to have concurred.

9. See Henry Kissinger, *Years of Upheaval* (Little, Brown, 1982), pp. 601–11.

Kissinger's role during the October war helped to persuade Sadat that the United States was prepared for a serious relationship, but it was the first phase of Kissinger's famous shuttle diplomacy that led to the flowering of the relationship. Initially Sadat was eager to get the Israelis to withdraw to the cease-fire lines of October 22, which would have provided relief for his encircled Third Army. Kissinger undertook to deal with the immediate problem of keeping the Third Army resupplied, but argued for a more ambitious, if delayed, first step.

Instead of haggling with the Israelis over the location of the October 22 lines, Kissinger suggested, why not aim for a more substantial disengagement of forces that would get the Israelis off the west bank of the canal entirely? This might permit the clearing of the canal and its quick return to use. Moreover, a disengagement agreement could be used to demonstrate that Israeli forces could be withdrawn from occupied territory through negotiations. Kissinger was eager to show that the United States could deliver results, and Sadat agreed to help Kissinger accomplish this goal. Thus began a process of near collusion in the peace negotiations that eventually produced four Egyptian-Israeli agreements between 1974 and 1979.

If Kissinger was the architect on the American side of the U.S.-Egyptian relationship, then Jimmy Carter was the inheritor and custodian of the special link to Sadat. After Carter became president in 1977, the two men developed an easy, cordial relationship. Carter, along with his secretary of state, Cyrus R. Vance, invested vast amounts of time and energy in Arab-Israeli diplomacy. In pursuit of an Egyptian-Israeli peace, Carter met personally with Sadat on four separate occasions in two years, twice in Egypt. Vance had an additional six meetings with Sadat, all in Egypt. Personal letters and telephone contacts were also a common occurrence. Sadat seemed to thrive on the special attention he received from Washington.

Inevitably, some of the intensity of the relationship began to subside once the Egyptian-Israeli peace treaty was signed in March 1979. Carter was obliged to turn his attention to other matters, including his reelection campaign and, from November 1979 on, the American hostages held in Tehran. Vance resigned in the spring of 1980. Carter's defeat in the November 1980 elections disappointed Sadat. He had no knowledge of the new president, Ronald Reagan, and little confidence in the new secretary of state, Alexander M. Haig, Jr.

Insofar as Reagan's views on Arab-Israeli issues were known at all, they seemed pro-Israeli. For example, in a piece published in the *Washington Post* on August 15, 1979, a year before he was elected president, Reagan had spoken of Israel as the only strategic asset in the Middle East region on which the United States could rely. "Specific Arab states such as Egypt— friendly to us at a particular moment—may well be able and prepared to take a front-line position in defense of Western security interests. To the extent that one or more can participate, so much the better; but such secondary links cannot substitute for a strong Israel in the ever-turbulent Middle East." This statement was a far cry from Sadat's view that Washington should accord Egypt equal treatment with Israel.

Haig's views seemed to revolve around the notion of forging an anti-Soviet "strategic consensus" in the region. It was not clear what this concept meant, but it did not seem to bode well for those who hoped to see the United States reassert itself as peace broker in the region. In fact, the Reagan administration hardly mentioned the Camp David Accords, perhaps because they were so closely associated with the Carter presidency. In any event, during 1981 and early 1982 the peace process, which had been such a strong element of the U.S.-Egyptian relationship under Nixon and Carter, got short shrift.

Haig also seemed to worry that Egypt might return to the Arab fold once it recovered Sinai from Israel in the spring of

1982.[10] When his concern was leaked to the press, it fed Egyptian fears that the strategy behind American peacemaking all along had been to split Egypt off from the other Arabs so that Israel could then absorb the other occupied territories—the West Bank and Gaza—without any serious Arab challenge. Once again, such a strategy was a far cry from the comprehensive peace that many Egyptians sincerely hoped the Americans would help to achieve.

Sadat's assassination in October 1981 necessarily affected the relationship between Cairo and Washington in subtle ways. In the minds of many Americans Sadat had been the personification of the new relationship with Egypt. He had courted the American press and Congress with great success. Public opinion polls showed that he was more popular with Americans than the Israeli leader Menachem Begin, and in 1979, at least, most Americans viewed Egypt as being equally important to the United States as Israel.[11]

Sadat's successor, Husni Mubarak, was less inclined to draw attention to the special relationship with Washington. By temperament he was a cautious leader, less flamboyant than Sadat and not given to theatrics. He also seemed to be eager to open up the Egyptian political system as a way of building his own legitimacy, so that Egyptian public opinion would probably influence his thinking more than it did Sadat's. Among intellectuals and within the political elite, opinion was still cool toward close alignment with any outside power. Israel was generally viewed as an adversary. And there was a distinct nostalgia for Egypt's Arab vocation. This feeling was shared,

10. See Bob Woodward, "Meetings' Notes Show the Unvarnished Haig," *Washington Post*, February 19, 1982, p. A14, where Secretary of State Haig expresses his concern that "Egypt is slipping back into [the] Arab world."

11. See John E. Rielly, ed., "American Public Opinion and U.S. Foreign Policy 1979" (Chicago: Council on Foreign Relations, 1979), pp. 16, 19.

though from a different perspective, by the Islamic current that was gaining ground at the popular level.

The Israeli invasion of Lebanon in June 1982, a watershed event in the Middle East, also created strains in U.S.-Egyptian relations.[12] For many Egyptians the United States had gone from being a full partner in the peace process to being a limited partner, if not a full-fledged accomplice, in the Israeli invasion and occupation of another Arab country. The chilling effect on U.S.-Arab relations generally was one of the reasons the Reagan administration decided to launch a new peace initiative. Reagan's speech on September 1, 1982, though not entirely welcome to most Arabs, at least put Washington back in the business of promoting a peace effort that called for eventual Israeli withdrawal from occupied Arab territory.[13] (Unfortunately for U.S.-Egyptian relations, the Reagan initiative never quite got off the ground. By the spring of 1983 King Hussein of Jordan had turned his back on it. And because 1984 was an American presidential election year, little movement could be expected until at least 1985.)

Reagan's reelection was for the most part welcomed in the Arab world. For all of their past disappointments with Reagan, Arabs now hoped to see a new face on Reagan's policy. Domestic pressures would presumably have less effect on a president who did not have to worry about running for reelection. Egypt therefore worked hard to forge a moderate Arab coali-

12. Quandt, ed., *Middle East*, pp. 9–10.
13. President Reagan's September 1, 1982, speech broke little new ground. Reagan did, however, say that the United States would "not support" the establishment of an independent Palestinian state in the West Bank and Gaza and would "not support" annexation or permanent control by Israel of those territories. Reagan went on to say that "it is the firm view of the United States that self-government by the Palestinians of the West Bank and Gaza in association with Jordan offers the best chance for a durable, just and lasting peace." See text and additional talking points in Quandt, ed., *Middle East*, pp. 461–70; quotation on p. 466.

tion, the centerpiece of the strategy being a rapprochement between Jordan and the Palestine Liberation Organization (PLO). That was achieved on February 11, 1985, with the signing of a joint statement outlining an approach to peace. Mubarak strongly supported this initiative and lobbied in Washington to encourage a positive response.

By the time King Hussein arrived in Washington in May 1985, the stage seemed to be set for the Reagan administration's return to the peacemaking game. But Reagan and his current secretary of state, George P. Shultz, balked; Congress held back on arms commitments to Jordan; and events intervened to spoil the atmosphere.

The event that brought the hesitant momentum in the peace process to a halt in October 1985 was the *Achille Lauro* affair. It also had a profoundly negative effect on U.S-Egyptian relations.

The *Achille Lauro* was an Italian cruise ship. On October 7, 1985, it was seized off the coast of Egypt by armed Palestinians from the Palestine Liberation Front, a small faction within the PLO led by Muhammad Abbas. The original plan may well have been to hold the passengers, many of whom were Americans, as hostages with the intention of exchanging them for Palestinian prisoners held in Israeli jails. While off the coast of Syria, however, the gunmen shot and killed a wheelchair-bound American, Leon Klinghoffer, and threw his body overboard. Shortly thereafter, Abbas ordered the terrorists to abandon their operation and head for Port Said on the Egyptian coast. After consulting with several governments, including the United States, the Egyptians agreed to let the ship dock in Port Said, where they took custody of the hijackers. Only several hours after the ship had docked was it learned for certain that one of the passengers had been killed.[14] By then, the Egyptians

14. See David C. Martin and John Walcott, *Best Laid Plans: The Inside Story of America's War against Terrorism* (Harper and Row, 1988), pp. 235–44.

had spirited the hijackers away, with the expressed intention of sending them to Tunis to be put on trial by the PLO.[15] When pressed by the Americans to reveal their whereabouts, the Egyptians said they had already left the country.

During the confusing few days following the Egyptian intervention in the *Achille Lauro* affair, American officials became convinced that Mubarak was being less than forthright in his answers concerning the whereabouts of the hijackers.[16] On October 10 an EgyptAir plane that had left Cairo for Tunis with the terrorists on board was intercepted by American F-14 fighters over the Mediterranean and forced to land at a NATO air base in Sicily. President Reagan, almost in jest, hinted that the plane might have been shot down had it not complied.[17] American public opinion seemed to be delighted that, for once, an antiterrorist operation had succeeded.

The Egyptians, who felt they had helped to save American lives by their involvement, resented both the lack of any expression of thanks by Reagan for their help and, especially, the gleeful way in which the Americans forced down the Egyptian plane. No other friendly country, they professed to believe, would be treated this way by the Americans. In Washington, by contrast, there was genuine outrage at the killing of Klinghoffer, irritation at Mubarak for being less than candid about the hijackers, and a determination not to let the terrorists get away. With such strong feelings on both sides, it was no surprise that mutual recriminations filled the press and airwaves. In political terms U.S.-Egyptian relations hit a low point. Only the passage of time helped ease some of the irritation that ensued.

15. Initially, President Reagan did not seem to object if Egypt sent the hijackers to Tunis to face trial by the PLO. See his comments as quoted by George de Lama, "U.S. Intercepts Pirates: Getaway Jet Lands in Italy," *Chicago Tribune*, October 11, 1985, p. 11; see also Mubarak's statement in *Time*, October 28, 1985, p. 26.

16. Martin and Walcott, *Best Laid Plans*, p. 244; and Bob Woodward, *Veil: The Secret Wars of the CIA, 1981–1987* (Simon and Schuster, 1987), pp. 414–16.

17. Lou Cannon, "President Basks in Praise: Hill Critics Join in Applauding 'Message to Terrorists,'" *Washington Post*, October 12, 1985, p. A20.

The *Achille Lauro* affair served to sabotage whatever slender chance there might have been in late 1985 of serious American involvement in the Jordanian-PLO peace initiative. King Hussein was already visibly moving into the Syrian camp, and by February 1986 he had broken off talks with Yasir Arafat, chairman of the PLO. These events did not end the diplomatic maneuvering over Arab-Israeli peace. But in the next phase Egypt was largely on the sidelines.

One idea closely identified with Egypt did, however, begin to win support; namely, an international conference on Middle East peace. Israel's prime minister, and later foreign minister, Shimon Peres, began to edge toward accepting some form of international conference as an umbrella under which direct negotiations between Israelis and Palestinians should take place. American interest in the same idea was soon forthcoming. In the course of 1986 and early 1987 the United States worked quietly, and with some results, to bring about an agreement between Peres and King Hussein on how to begin peace talks. In April 1987 the parties concurred on the so-called London Document, a set of procedures for convening and conducting negotiations under the auspices of an international conference.[18]

Though Egyptians were pleased to see the evolution of American policy on the international conference, they were also annoyed at not being kept in the picture. Hussein was consulting more often with Syria's president, Hafiz al-Asad, than with them. And Asad was saying that Egypt would not even be present at an international conference, since it had already made peace with Israel.

Despite some qualms about being on the sidelines, the Egyptians were hopeful the United States would lend its weight to the idea of convening a conference. Because Yitzhak Shamir, who had replaced Peres as prime minister in 1986, was outspo-

18. Text in Quandt, ed., *Middle East*, pp. 475–76.

kenly against the idea, it was widely assumed that Israel might face a cabinet crisis over this issue. Optimists in Washington and Cairo hoped that Peres might use the crisis to force new elections that would return him to power. But George Shultz was unwilling to be drawn into the domestic Israeli political arena in such an obvious manner. He endorsed the London Document only lukewarmly. Shamir rejected it, and that was that; Peres had nowhere else to turn.

The Egyptians were disappointed with the apparent collapse of the effort to convene an international conference in the spring of 1987. Nor were they overjoyed with Washington's next move in October. Shultz, while in Israel en route to Moscow to prepare for the Reagan-Gorbachev summit, floated the idea of having the two superpowers call on Hussein and Shamir to enter into direct negotiations. In fact, both leaders might be invited to the Washington superpower summit. Shamir was cautiously positive about the idea. Hussein, who was about to host a meeting of the Arab League in Amman, was both surprised by the idea and unable to respond positively. The Egyptians, once again, felt they were being neglected as Washington crafted its moves in the Middle East without consulting them.

At the time of the signing of the Egyptian-Israeli peace treaty in 1979, the United States had undertaken a commitment to help to ensure compliance with the treaty.[19] The United States therefore became involved in the resolution of the one remaining territorial dispute between Egypt and Israel, that over a tiny strip of land in northeastern Sinai called Taba. The peace treaty called for disputes to be resolved by negotiation. If that failed, disputes were to be resolved by conciliation or submitted to arbitration (article 7). Washington made little effort to hide its belief that Egypt was in the right on Taba, but it nonetheless was reluctant to recommend binding arbitration until all other

19. Text in Quandt, *Camp David*, p. 406.

avenues had clearly been exhausted. The case did finally go to arbitration and was settled in Egypt's favor. That the treaty had been observed and that it had served Egyptian interests were a plus for Mubarak and gave a boost to U.S.-Egyptian relations as well.

Another treaty-related issue, however, had the potential for becoming more controversial. Article 6 of the treaty dealt with the so-called priority of obligations, which was meant to deal with possible conflicts between the Egyptian-Israeli treaty and other treaty commitments of the parties. Egypt's commitments under the Arab Defense Pact of the early 1950s were of particular concern.

During the negotiations in early 1979 Egypt had asked for an American legal finding on whether, without violating the peace treaty with Israel, Egypt could send troops to help defend an Arab country that had been attacked by Israel. In a preliminary legal opinion the State Department said yes. The Israelis were furious and asked for a letter from the United States that would make clear that it did not view Israel's occupation of Arab territory as constituting aggression. Once again, the United States complied and sent a letter stating its agreement with this Israeli position, which made the Egyptians furious. Finally, the United States decided to withdraw both the initial legal opinion and the interpretive letter to Israel. Neither was considered to have any legal validity.

Early in 1988, however, as Egypt was beginning to restore its relations with one Arab country after another, the Egyptians put out the word that the Americans had given them a legal finding permitting them to come to the defense of any Arab country under attack from Israel. They repeated this message on many occasions, but it aroused little interest in Israel or the United States.[20] Still, it indicated a potential divergence in in-

---

20. See interview with Usamah al-Baz, an adviser to Mubarak, *Al-Siyasah* (Kuwait), January 5, 1988, p. 9, in Foreign Broadcast Information Service, *Daily*

terpreting the treaty, since the essential American position is that the Egyptian-Israeli treaty does in fact prevail over other previous Egyptian commitments, though it does allow for the right of self-defense as guaranteed by the UN Charter.

If Arab-Israeli issues were often the most direct source of irritants in U.S.-Egyptian relations, they were not the only ones in the last two years of the Reagan administration. Mubarak had always suspected the United States of secretly colluding with Israel and other countries to help Iran in its war against Iraq. Most of the evidence for such charges was circumstantial—until the fall of 1986, when the White House revealed that arms had been sold to Iran during the previous year in order to try to win the release of American hostages in Lebanon. Israel, it soon became clear, was intimately involved in the supply of arms to Iran at the behest of the United States, just as Mubarak had always suspected. Shultz had opposed the policy, but Reagan had gone along with the scheme. Throughout the Arab world, American credibility was badly damaged. It was only during 1987 and 1988, with the clear commitment of American naval ships to protect Kuwaiti oil tankers threatened by Iran, that U.S.-Arab relations generally began to improve.

It says something about the maturity of Egyptian-American relations that a series of potentially damaging incidents—the Israeli invasion of Lebanon, the *Achille Lauro* affair, the arms sales to Iran—as well as the widespread Egyptian perception that Reagan and Shultz were biased in favor of Israel did not do lasting damage to the ties between Cairo and Washington. Both parties preferred to contain problems as they arose. So they were still able to cooperate in efforts to resume the peace process in late 1988, when the Reagan administration, to the

---

Report: Near East and South Asia, January 12, 1988, pp. 25–26. (Hereafter FBIS, *NESA.*)

surprise of many, showed a willingness to open a dialogue with the PLO.

Mubarak had long urged Washington to deal with Yasir Arafat, whom he termed a moderate leader. But this advice had fallen on deaf ears in Washington. Instead, Shultz decided in the spring of 1988 to launch an initiative centered on Jordan and the convening of an international conference. Mubarak was largely supportive of this effort, but within a few months it was clear that Prime Minister Shamir was adamant in his refusal to accept the plan's main provisions. Most observers then concluded that nothing more could be expected from the lame duck Reagan administration.

Shultz and his advisers eventually came to realize that a flaw in their plan was that it provided little incentive for Palestinian participation. And without that, King Hussein could not move. This, in essence, was what the king said in his speech on July 31, 1988, when he announced the end of Jordan's administrative and legal ties to the West Bank and placed full responsibility for recovering the occupied territories in the hands of the PLO. Within days of the king's announcement, Shultz signaled to the PLO that the United States would be prepared to open an official dialogue with it, provided that three conditions were met: acceptance of UN Resolutions 242 and 338, which would have the effect of committing the PLO to seek a peaceful resolution of the conflict with Israel through negotiations; recognition of Israel's right to exist; and renunciation of terrorism.[21]

During the ensuing months the Egyptians worked closely with the PLO to help Arafat move toward meeting the Ameri-

21. The first of these two conditions—acceptance of UN Resolutions 242 and 338 and recognition of Israel's right to exist—were set down in a "Memorandum of Agreement" signed by Secretary of State Henry A. Kissinger and Israeli Foreign Minister Yigal Allon on September 1, 1975. The third condition—that the PLO renounce terrorism—was included in legislation passed by Congress in 1985. See *Legislation on Foreign Relations through 1986*, vol. 1: *Current Legislation and Related Executive Orders*, S. Prt. 100–21 (Government Printing Office, 1987), pp. 359–60.

can conditions. Washington welcomed the Egyptian role, although it did not rely primarily on Cairo as an intermediary with Arafat. By late November it seemed as if nothing would come of the effort to bridge the American-PLO gap. Shultz, though he had refused to grant Arafat a visa to come to New York to address the UN General Assembly, was in touch with the PLO through the Swedish government to explore the possibility of clinching a deal before the end of the Reagan administration. In the end Arafat uttered the magic words on December 14, 1988, in Geneva, and Shultz responded by recommending to Reagan that he authorize the beginning of official talks with the PLO. The Egyptians had weighed in with both parties at the last minute, and Washington and Cairo were pleased with the result. Thus the Reaganites left office with a legacy of goodwill in Cairo.

President George Bush and his secretary of state, James A. Baker III, were viewed positively by officials in Cairo. There was a widespread perception that they would be more committed to promoting a peace settlement than Reagan and Shultz had been. Some of the impression may have been little more than wishful thinking, but it did indicate how much the Egyptian establishment counted on the United States to show leadership in promoting the peace process.

A sign of the continuing close relations between Washington and Cairo was the fact that President Mubarak was one of the first foreign leaders to come to Washington after President Bush's inauguration. His April 1989 visit concentrated on two points: reviving the peace process under American leadership and providing debt relief for Egypt's ailing economy. On the first point, Mubarak had to be satisfied with a number of statements made by the new administration that suggested a serious approach toward the peace process. For example, President Bush spoke of the need to end the Israeli occupation as part of an overall settlement.[22] The administration took no immediate action on the debt problem, however, although by some sleight of hand it discovered that Egypt could count some previously unknown payments against debts coming due in the summer of 1989, so that the Brooke Amendment would not be triggered.[23] Time was thereby gained during which it might be possible to reschedule debt payments once again. But despite some Egyptian hopes in advance of the visit, no progress was made on waiving debt repayment or releasing the cash component of aid that was being withheld pending the completion of a plan for Egyptian economic reforms.[24] Thus, from the Egyptian standpoint, the first high-level encounter with the Bush administration produced mixed results.

As Mubarak's visit to Washington demonstrated, Cairo finds itself in a somewhat awkward position with regard to the peace process. It has not always been a full partner with the United States in trying to revive the peace effort, although extensive cooperation has taken place since mid-1989. Its Arab concerns, and the importance of its relations with the PLO, affect its position in ways that differ from Washington's views. Nor has Cairo had much influence in Israel. Its demarches have often been ignored, its trial balloons allowed to drift aimlessly until they pop. Arafat has visited Cairo regularly and Egyptian-

22. Meeting with Mubarak on April 3, 1989, Bush said, "Egypt and the United States share the goals of security for Israel, the end of occupation, and the achievement of Palestinian political rights." Thomas L. Friedman, "Bush Urges Israel to End Occupation of Arab Territory," *New York Times*, April 4, 1989, p. A1.

23. The Brooke Amendment stipulates that any country which falls behind in its debt repayments to the U.S. government by more than one year will no longer be eligible to receive new assistance.

24. In August 1989, $115 million in cash from the fiscal 1988 program was finally released. See "U.S. Thaws Aid to Egypt," *Washington Post*, August 18, 1989, p. A26.

PLO ties have been strong, but Egypt cannot easily serve as an intermediary between Israel and the PLO because the Likud bloc, Israel's right-wing party, wants to have nothing to do with Arafat and his organization. And now that the PLO and Washington are on speaking terms, Cairo has less of a role to play there as well. Still, as the course of Arab-Israeli diplomacy from mid-1989 demonstrated, the United States, Israel, and the PLO may all find it convenient for Egypt to "front" for the Palestinians in exploring different procedural devices to get Israeli-Palestinian talks started. On occasion, the Bush administration has even concluded that it is more productive to have Egypt deal with the PLO directly than to use the official U.S.-PLO channel now available.

Despite Egyptian frustrations over the peace process, Egypt's foreign policy establishment does not want to wash its hands of the Palestinian issue. On the contrary, the peace process still has a high priority on the Egyptian agenda, and Egypt hopes to take an important part in resolving it at some point. Egypt is, after all, now on reasonably good terms with all the parties to the conflict.[25]

The point of this discussion is to serve as a reminder that the peace process remains an issue in U.S.-Egyptian relations. It is still a source of strength in the relationship, especially when Washington and Cairo are coordinating their efforts, but it can

25. One can legitimately question whether the achievement of a comprehensive peace might set the stage for reducing the levels of U.S. aid to Egypt, since it would no longer be necessary to "reward" Egypt for helping with the peace process. But even though its moods cannot be easily predicted, Congress would be unlikely to cut aid to an Egypt that had helped bring about a comprehensive peace and that was living up to its obligations under the peace treaty with Israel. After all, there would always be the danger that the peace agreements could unravel. The United States would almost certainly want to continue paying an "insurance premium" in the form of aid to reduce such risks. In brief, Egypt can be a valuable partner for the United States during peace negotiations and after agreements are reached. Unfortunately, it seems unlikely that a comprehensive settlement is in the offing, and therefore this issue will remain a matter for speculation.

also be a source of great frustration, especially when no real movement is occurring or when one party begins to doubt the good faith of the other.

The special advantages associated with an Egyptian role in the peace process should not be ignored. Unlike other Arab states, Egypt has no conflict of interest in principle with the idea of a Palestinian state. Jordan and Syria will always be seen by the PLO as competitors, at least to some extent, whereas Egypt has no ideological or material reasons to oppose the PLO's central goal. Egypt, unlike most other Arab states, has not tried in recent years to co-opt part of the PLO and bring it under direct control. More important, Egypt needs the PLO in a way other Arab states do not. For Egypt to be seen as supporting the PLO is good domestic politics, particularly in light of criticisms of the regime from both right and left. Furthermore, movement in the peace process would help to vindicate Egypt's argument that its own peace agreement with Israel was not at the expense of the Palestinians.

Both Washington and Cairo realize they will not always see eye-to-eye on issues of Arab-Israeli peace. The United States seems wedded to its strong support for Israel, and Egypt seems to accept the fact that it cannot drive a wedge between the two countries. Washington apparently understands that Egypt is set to resume a major role in inter-Arab affairs, but that it will not do so at the expense of either the treaty with Israel or the relationship with Washington.

As of 1990, the peace process still has a central part in making American-Egyptian political ties special. Without it, a heavy burden would be carried by the security and economic elements of the relationship, both of which are subject to periodic difficulties.

Security and Military Issues

If the political and diplomatic dialogue between Egypt and the United States was the leavening for the relationship in its early years, more recently security has provided enduring sustenance. While giving tangible benefits to both parties, the security relationship is nonetheless potentially troubled. More than any other aspect of U.S.-Egyptian relations, security cooperation depends on continued peace between Egypt and Israel. The American supply of arms to Egypt could never have begun on a large scale until peace was achieved, and it could not continue if Egypt were to return to a posture of belligerency toward Israel.

Furthermore, the security relationship between the United States and Egypt is likely to change as the cold war rationale for military assistance begins to fade. In a post–cold war Middle East, neither Egypt nor Israel can expect to present themselves credibly as important "strategic assets" in confronting a waning Soviet threat. More to the point, Congress may tire of paying out large sums for military assistance in the 1990s. As a result, the U.S.-Egyptian security relationship will be subject to careful scrutiny in the years ahead.

At its core, the security link consists of the provision of some $1.3 billion each year for Egypt to purchase American arms. Since the start of the program in 1979, Egypt has purchased about $13 billion worth of arms, including F-16 aircraft, and has acquired production rights to the M-1 tank.[26] The United

26. The eventual cost of the M-1 program, if it is completed, will probably exceed $2 billion. See Patrick E. Tyler, "Pentagon Agrees to Let Egypt Produce M1 Tank," *Washington Post,* June 29, 1987, pp. A1, A16, and "Egypt May Drop Plans for U.S. Tank," *Washington Post,* May 12, 1989, pp. A25, A28; and Robert

States supplied nearly 40 percent of the new equipment purchased in the first half of the 1980s by the Egyptian military.[27] Were foreign military sales (FMS) credits no longer approved by Congress, this percentage would drop sharply, since without them American equipment would be comparatively expensive.

Besides selling arms to Egypt, the United States provides training for Egyptian officers, holds joint exercises with Egyptian forces, exchanges intelligence, and carries out some cooperative security programs. For example, the American program of providing arms to the Afghan *mujahideen* was assisted logistically by Egypt, as was the unsuccessful attempt in early 1980 to rescue the American hostages held in Tehran. In pursuit of some of these common objectives, Egypt has granted the United States selective access to military facilities and has allowed pre-positioning of some military equipment. This arrangement, however, has stopped short of the development of sovereign American bases on Egyptian soil.[28]

On balance, both Washington and Cairo express satisfaction with the security element of the bilateral relationship.[29] Given the role of the Egyptian military as a prime support for the

---

Pear, "White House Seeks Increase in Sales of Arms Overseas," *New York Times*, May 2, 1988, pp. A1, A8.

27. Robert B. Satloff, *Army and Politics in Mubarak's Egypt*, Policy Papers Number Ten (Washington Institute for Near East Policy, 1988), p. 9, citing the U.S. Arms Control and Disarmament Agency.

28. Although the United States has no military bases in Egypt, it has sometimes been able to arrange for "access" to military facilities, especially at Cairo West airport and the airbase at Wadi Qena. See the report in Richard Halloran, "U.S. Tells of Secret Air Operations in Egypt," *New York Times*, June 24, 1983, p. A9, referring to a "secret base" in Egypt; and Walter Pincus and Fred Hiatt, "U.S. Has a Secret Base with 100 Men in Egypt," *Washington Post*, June 23, 1983, p. A2.

29. Some observers attributed the relatively stable and cordial U.S.-Egyptian relationship in the military and security arena to the fact that the Egyptian ministry of defense remained under the control of Field Marshal Abd al-Halim Abu Ghazaleh for most of this period. But his sudden departure on April 15, 1989, did not seem to disrupt the bilateral relationship in any significant way.

regime, both Presidents Sadat and Mubarak have been eager
to obtain arms from the United States. After the break with the
Soviet Union, in particular, the regime needed to show the military that the shift in alliances would not be detrimental to
Egypt's security or to the prestige of the armed forces. Thus a
regular flow of sophisticated weapons has been important to
the civilian leaders in Cairo, irrespective of any immediate
threats from beyond Egypt's borders. The United States has
usually been responsive, although quarrels have arisen over
delivery schedules and costs.[30]

For the United States, the provision of security assistance to
Egypt has entailed some real benefits. Early on, the United
States was given access to most of the Soviet equipment in the
Egyptian arsenal. (The Mig-23 aircraft was of special interest.)
In exchange, the United States helped provide Egypt with the
means to keep its Soviet fleet of aircraft in operation without
having to rely on the Soviets for technical aid or spare parts.

Perhaps of greater long-term importance, the United States
was able to develop a working relationship with a whole co-
hort of Egyptian military officers, men who had previously received the bulk of their training in the Soviet Union. One can
never be sure of the political effects of such contacts, but there
is no reason to think that Egyptian officers are politically anti-
American as a result of their experiences. Since the Egyptian
military plays a political role, it is presumably useful for the
United States to have these contacts.[31]

The American involvement with Egypt's security has also
clearly reduced the risk of hostilities between Egypt and Israel.

30. In 1988 Congress waived some nonrecurrent and administrative charges
for purchasing F-16 aircraft for both Israel and Egypt. This saved Egypt about $50
million. See Leonard B. Zuza, "A Paper Examining Selected Options for Enhanc-
ing the Effectiveness of Security Assistance," February 14, 1989, p. 8.

31. Some have speculated that Field Marshal Abu Ghazaleh was removed
from his position as minister of defense because he was too closely identified with
the Americans. But many other explanations have also been put forward, and the
American connection does not seem to me to have been decisive.

From the time of the early disengagement agreements of the mid-1970s onward, the United States has helped to monitor force deployments in Sinai. After the final withdrawal of Israeli forces from Sinai in the spring of 1982, the United States contributed to a multinational force to supervise the limitations on military deployments as stipulated in the peace treaty. Egyptians and Israelis, one senses, feel less need to prepare for the contingency of hostilities on the Egyptian-Israeli front because of the American presence as a buffer between them.

Part of the military relationship between the two countries is genuinely intended to deal with Egyptian security problems. But no one can deny that political and symbolic purposes are also being served. Egypt wants the prestige of having access to sophisticated equipment and technology. For some Egyptians, it is also important that they and the Israelis be seen as receiving comparable treatment from the United States. Thus some Egyptians were pleased at the implied equality of status in the U.S. decision to designate both Israel and Egypt as "non-NATO allies" for purposes of participating in research on the strategic defense initiative.

Despite the many pluses in the U.S.-Egyptian security relationship, problems are inevitable, some of which could become more important in the future. For example, one effect of the large infusion of American aid has been to swell the size and cost of the Egyptian armed forces. One might have assumed that after the peace treaty in 1979 Egypt would cut its forces. But with Mubarak's accession to power in October 1981, the size of the armed forces increased, though the number of front-line combat units has probably not grown significantly. Many of those counted as part of the armed forces are reservists or are carrying out semicivilian tasks.[32] Still, the military remains

32. Some of these civilian activities may not be helpful to the economy as a whole. For example, low-cost labor provided by the military may produce food or goods that are dumped on the local market, thereby undercutting efforts by private entrepreneurs who do not enjoy subsidized labor costs.

a large factor in Egyptian society, so that a sizable share of Egypt's economic resources is being devoted to it. American aid does not cover all these costs by any means, since it is essentially used to finance the purchase of American equipment. Over time, the size of Egypt's military budget could retard Egypt's economic development.[33]

The Egyptian military has indeed become a major force in the economy of Egypt. It controls significant sectors of the economy and has become largely autonomous, running its own industries, growing its own food, and providing its own housing. This rather privileged sector of society may contribute to regime stability, or it may become a praetorian guard in the future. In any event, Egypt's leaders have to be keenly aware of the military as they experiment with democratization.

Egypt's military development in the 1980s could not have progressed so rapidly had it not been for the infusion of the more than $1 billion of annual American aid to purchase arms. Since fiscal year 1985 all this aid has been provided on a grant basis, which the Egyptians appreciate.[34] Nonetheless, as suggested earlier, military relations between Cairo and Washington have at times been troubled and there are issues on the horizon that could cause problems.

Egyptians inevitably complain about the cost of American weapons even though the expense is covered by FMS grants.

33. See Arms Control and Disarmament Agency, *World Military Expenditures and Arms Transfers, 1987* (Washington, D.C., 1988), p. 57. According to these figures, Egypt's military expenditures in 1985 amounted to 14.2 percent of GNP and 28.1 percent of central government expenditures. Military expenditures per capita, in 1984 constant dollars, came to $124. Out of 144 countries studied by ACDA, Egypt ranked number 11 in terms of military expenditures as a percent of GNP (p. 32). Despite the size of military spending in Egypt, the International Monetary Fund has not put much pressure on the government to cut this part of the budget, perhaps because much of the ministry of defense expenditures are considered to be "off-budget."

34. A heavy legacy of debt from the FMS program between fiscal years 1979 and 1984 affects the economic relationship and is discussed in the next section.

They feel they should get more for the amounts spent. Occasionally, disagreements arise over delivery schedules and over the quality of the equipment that Egypt will be allowed to purchase. Ever since Egypt's peace treaty with Israel, Congress has been relatively receptive to arms sales to Egypt, but that attitude could change, particularly if the weapons requested were seen as constituting a possible threat to Israel. Also, if the U.S.-Soviet rivalry in the region does subside, Congress and the administration may be reluctant to subsidize a costly arms buildup in the Middle East.

In the past, and possibly again in the future, there have been problems associated with American military activities that seem to infringe on Egyptian sovereignty. For example, the United States has sought permission for nuclear-powered aircraft carriers to pass through the Suez Canal, but Egypt has balked at such requests. At times, too, the Egyptian press has criticized the presence of American military personnel at certain Egyptian bases, implying that Egypt is forfeiting its sovereignty by allowing Americans to remain on them. During the early 1980s Egyptians resented U.S. pressures to develop and gain access to the base at Ras Banas on the Red Sea. On the whole, however, these issues have remained manageable. The Egyptian government is still convinced that it benefits from this aspect of the relationship with the United States.

In 1988–89 two security-related issues arose that held the potential of damaging U.S.-Egyptian relations. One was the report that Egypt was building a large chemical weapons factory.[35] In light of the Iraqi use of chemical weapons during the war with Iran, and reports that Libya was also developing a chemical weapons capability, it would not be surprising if Egypt were to expand its modest chemical warfare capacity.

35. Michael R. Gordon, with Stephen Engelberg, "Egypt Accused of Big Advance on Poison Gas," *New York Times*, March 10, 1989, pp. A1, A12.

But the timing and the clandestine nature of the project raised sharp concern in Washington.[36]

A second troubling issue was evidence that Egypt was secretly trying to acquire elements that might be used to produce warheads for ballistic missiles. According to American court reports, Egyptian officials sought a certain carbon compound that was banned for export and that had potential use in a sophisticated missile program. Egypt denied the charges, and an effort was made to keep the issue from damaging bilateral relations, but continued activity of that kind would raise serious questions in Washington.[37]

Despite these problems, the military relationship has remained strong over the years. But it depends almost entirely on the continuation of a large FMS grant program, without which Egypt would be obliged to seek Arab funds to purchase U.S. weapons, or would be forced to turn to alternative sources of supply for its military. For the moment the FMS program appears to enjoy solid support in Congress, and therefore the relationship is not at risk. But it may well become necessary to think of reducing the FMS program both to help limit the disastrous effects of the large stock of FMS debt from an earlier era and to accommodate pressure for cuts in military aid more generally. A smaller program might still provide a firm foundation for military cooperation, but at some point Egypt could begin to feel slighted, especially if Israel continued to receive full funding for its programs.

The dilemma for the United States may well be that in order to help Egypt with its economic problems it may have to reduce military assistance. For Egypt, the choice would be diffi-

36. According to some sources, the former defense minister, Abu Ghazaleh, had kept President Mubarak in the dark concerning this project, which may have been one reason he lost his job.

37. See Patrick E. Tyler, "High Link Seen in Cairo Spy Case," *Washington Post*, August 20, 1988, pp. A1, A15, A16.

cult: would the country be better off with less indebtedness and a somewhat smaller military assistance program from Washington, or would any reduction in security assistance be seen as a threat to the regime's stability? These are the kinds of questions no one likes to ask, but it will be hard to get through the 1990s without addressing them in some form.

On balance, Americans are likely to conclude that economic issues will require more attention than issues of security assistance because of the relatively nonthreatening environment surrounding Egypt.

Economic Issues

Economic issues have had an ambiguous effect on U.S.-Egyptian relations. On the one hand, economic assistance has been a central element in the growth of ties between Egypt and the United States. President Sadat, who had little patience for economic discussions, seemed to assume that Washington would provide the solvent for his country's economic problems. Some observers believed a large-scale influx of capital, technology, and expertise was the key to Egypt's economic development. With peace, Egypt would presumably reap a prosperity dividend.

On the other hand, with aid came debt, both for economic projects and military purchases. And indebtedness has always been a sensitive issue in Egyptian politics ever since the British intervened in the late nineteenth century to protect creditors, and then proceeded to stay for some seventy years.[38] Aid and debt are related issues, but require separate analysis here.[39]

Aid

Despite the high hopes in the late 1970s that peace would lead to an economic boom in Egypt, optimism soon began to fade. The Egyptian economy, and with it the bilateral U.S.-Egyptian aid relationship, has had to struggle with the accumulated consequences of long-standing economic problems, aggravated by the sudden drop in oil revenues in the mid-

38. See, for example, Roger Owen, *The Middle East in the World Economy, 1800–1914* (Methuen, 1981), pp. 130–35.

39. An earlier analysis of these issues that reaches similar conclusions to mine is Paul Jabber, "Egypt's Crisis, America's Dilemma," *Foreign Affairs*, vol. 64 (Summer 1986), pp. 960–80.

1980s. Neither the Egyptians nor the Americans are satisfied with the existing situation, and economic issues are becoming increasingly divisive. A new look seems to be required for the 1990s.

Between fiscal years 1974 and 1990 the United States provided about $17 billion to Egypt in various forms of economic aid (see table A-1).[40] No country other than Israel received more. As mentioned earlier, Egypt was far ahead of such traditional American allies as Turkey, Pakistan, and the Philippines.

About three-quarters of all American economic aid has been provided through the economic support fund (ESF), most of which (79 percent) has come in the form of grants. (Since fiscal 1982 all ESF funds have been in grant form.) ESF money has gone to development projects (over 50 percent), the financing of commodity imports from the United States (about one-third), and direct cash transfers (less than 10 percent).[41]

Approximately 20 percent of American economic aid has taken the form of sales of wheat and agricultural products under Public Law 480. The terms of the sales are highly concessional, so that about 60 percent of the total program can be considered a grant. Slightly under 5 percent of economic assistance has taken the form of Export-Import Bank credits, although since fiscal 1985 this has been a tiny part of the whole program.

Egyptian complaints about the economic assistance program

40. Helpful overviews of the aid program can be found in Denis Joseph Sullivan, "American Economic Aid to Egypt, 1975–86: Political and Bureaucratic Struggles over AID Disbursement and Development Choices," Ph.D. dissertation, University of Michigan, 1987; Marvin G. Weinbaum, *Egypt and the Politics of U.S. Economic Aid* (Boulder, Colo.: Westview, 1986); and Roy L. Prosterman and Jeffrey M. Riedinger, *Egyptian Development and U.S. Aid: A 6-Year Report*, RDI Monographs in Foreign Aid and Development 2 (Seattle: Rural Development Institute, November 1985).

41. Statistics provided by the American Embassy in Cairo, summer 1987, "U.S. Economic Assistance to Egypt, 1975–1986."

begin with its size. Many Egyptians believe they were promised parity with Israel when they signed the Camp David Accords. But Israel, with a population of less than 10 percent that of Egypt, has received considerably more economic and military assistance, and on much better terms.[42] The Americans reply, correctly, that no formal promise of parity was ever made, despite informal comments by President Carter that Egypt—if only it made peace with the Jewish state—could expect to have the same kind of relationship with Washington that Israel had.

Egyptian officials have also complained about the content and structure of the economic aid program, administered by the Agency for International Development (AID). Experts themselves at bureaucratic delays, the Egyptians have found a worthy competitor in the AID bureaucracy, or so they seem to believe. At the outset of the program, the Egyptians were surprised that the large sums appropriated by Congress were slow in arriving. The delay was due both to the need for feasibility studies (often carried out by high-priced American consultants) and to the practice of disbursing project money only when work actually got under way. This created a so-called pipeline problem, much of which was eventually resolved as projects got started.

Egyptian officials were not always happy with the allocation of project aid. Some seemed to favor big projects, such as power stations, rather than less visible work in rural areas. Voices were raised, especially on the left and in academic circles, claiming that AID was taking over the Egyptian economy, pushing free enterprise ideas, and generally helping only the well-to-do sectors of society. The large AID presence in the

42. In fiscal 1989 Israel received more than $3 billion in economic and military assistance, all in the form of grants. Economic aid to Israel is all in the form of cash transfer, whereas only about 12 percent of such aid to Egypt takes that form.

country was also the target of criticism, particularly since AID personnel are paid much more than Egyptian bureaucrats.[43]

Few Egyptians would deny that some of the projects have produced beneficial results, especially those small projects proposed and implemented by Egyptians under the decentralization program. Good work has also been done in the countryside. But for every success story, such as telecommunications, power generation, and waste disposal, one hears of serious problems as well.

If Egyptians have expressed dissatisfaction with project aid, and have usually pleaded for more cash transfers, Congress also has been critical of AID in Egypt. From Washington's perspective, the problems look a bit different. No one on the Egyptian side seems willing to set economic priorities. Ministries battle with one another and make project implementation difficult, if not impossible. AID is often made a scapegoat by inefficient Egyptian bureaucrats. And, of course, Egyptians rarely express any gratitude for the substantial funds provided by hard-pressed American taxpayers. Were it not for the belief that the United States incurred an obligation to Egypt when the Camp David Accords were signed, Congress by now would surely have cut the program substantially.[44]

The issue of economic reform has also come to bedevil the bilateral U.S.-Egyptian economic relationship. For many years

43. See Earl L. Sullivan, "Conclusion: Foreign Aid and the Future of Egypt," *Cairo Papers in Social Science*, vol. 7, monograph 3 (September 1984), pp. 95–101; a critical article by Saad ad-Din Ibrahim, "An American Shadow Government in Cairo," *Al-Ahram al-Iqtisadi*, October 11, 1982, pp. 11–14; and Soheir A. Morsy, "U.S. Aid to Egypt: An Illustration and Account of U.S. Foreign Assistance Policy," *Arab Studies Quarterly*, vol. 8 (Fall 1986), pp. 358–89.

44. Some congressmen, such as David R. Obey, have talked of a 10 percent across-the-board cut in aid. If the "earmarked" security assistance accounts for Egypt and Israel were exempted from cuts, the full burden would fall on the remaining aid recipients, resulting in much larger percentage cuts. See Zuza, "Paper Examining Selected Options."

Egypt was reluctant to go to the International Monetary Fund and the World Bank for help. The reason was simple. The IMF, as a condition for help, insists on painful economic reforms, usually according to a fairly rigid formula. Egypt, after the riots of January 1977, sparked in large measure by increases in the price of bread, has been leery of following IMF guidelines. As long as oil revenues were pouring in as they were during the late 1970s and early 1980s, Egypt believed it could afford to forgo economic reform, using its large foreign currency flows to subsidize food imports and pay off loans.

Oil prices took a sharp downturn, however, in 1985–86. This decline has had direct and indirect effects on Egypt, since Suez Canal revenues and remittances from Egyptians working in the Gulf Arab countries were also linked to oil. Moreover, tourism dropped off in 1986 after a spate of terrorism in the Middle East. With mounting debt repayments to meet, Egypt could no longer afford to ignore the need for economic reform. Creditors would not agree to rescheduling unless good-faith efforts at reform were made. The so-called Paris Club of creditors (the major industrial countries) turned to the IMF to develop a reform package for Egypt. The understanding was explicit: there would be no rescheduling of outstanding debt repayments unless the IMF approved a "standby" agreement on reforms.

After much haggling, the IMF reached an agreement with Egypt in May 1987. The IMF agreed to make $325 million in loans available for balance-of-payments support. Soon thereafter the Paris Club agreed to reschedule payments due through mid-1988 on some $12 billion worth of civilian and military debt. These measures gave Egypt a breathing spell but did not solve the problem.[45]

45. Paul D. Morris, "Egypt's Economic Problems and Debt Repayment Prospects," parts 3 and 4, *Middle East Executive Reports*, vol. 10 (August 1987), p. 11, and (September 1987), p. 13. Only one-half of the IMF standby credits were

Optimists professed to believe that economic reform would help the Egyptian economy to grow and thus lessen the debt burden. Pessimists feared that the cure—price increases, devaluation, and higher interest rates—would be fatal to the patient, largely because of inflationary pressure and the political consequences in urban areas. Whenever riots occurred in a developing country, such as Algeria in October 1988, Venezuela in February 1989, and Jordan in April 1989, the Egyptians took note and told their creditors they could not move quickly toward a full liberalization of the economy.

The United States, having initially made aid commitments to Egypt in a thoroughly political context, increasingly found itself using aid as a lever to promote economic reform. For example, in both fiscal 1988 and fiscal 1989 the cash component of ESF, amounting to some $115 million each year, was withheld pending compliance with economic reforms. One congressman, normally friendly to Egypt, expressed exasperation, complaining that American taxpayers had poured billions of dollars into Egypt and received "nothing in return."[46] In an earlier era what the United States had received "in return" would have been obvious—the Egyptian-Israeli peace treaty—but that was now taken for granted.

The attempt to use aid as direct leverage to get Egypt to reform its economy has had mixed results. Echoing the IMF, some Americans argue that such reforms are for Egypt's own good and that without them the aid is much less effective. This growth-oriented school assumes that Egypt can master its economic problems through liberalization and privatization of the economy. Decisions on aid and debt relief should therefore be used as levers to move the Egyptians to take the decisions that

actually disbursed before the agreement broke down. A new standby agreement was under negotiation in early 1990.

46. Quoted in Patrick E. Tyler, "Mubarak Seeks Easing Doubts on Poison Gas, Aid during U.S. Visit," *Washington Post*, April 1, 1989, p. A18.

will ultimately be for their own good. Proponents of this view argue that past failures to produce reforms have resulted from the tentativeness of U.S. efforts. A harder push is required. At a time when some countries in central Europe are rapidly moving toward reform, Congress will be unsympathetic with hesitant efforts to overhaul ailing economies.

This interventionist and manipulative approach is risky, however, since the United States can become a scapegoat if growth fails to take place. But the alternative is seen by the growth strategists as even riskier: the Egyptian economy will stagnate, Congress will tire of pouring good money after bad, and eventually even debt relief will do little to help Egypt avoid a crushing repetition of the cycle of dependence, intervention, and frustration with some new creditor—if any such creditor can be found.

Many who have carefully studied the Egyptian case tend to roll their eyes in disbelief when well-meaning congressmen and bureaucrats talk about pressuring the Egyptians to shape up their economy along liberal, free-enterprise lines. They argue that American aid cannot be decisive in bolstering the long-term viability of the Egyptian economy, and that care must be taken not to exacerbate Egypt's economic problems by poorly conceived programs.

Even those with modest expectations about economic assistance in the Egyptian context are willing to admit that aid can sometimes be useful. For example, when certain economic reforms are being instituted, the government may need to ease the transition by continuing substantial imports until the beneficial effects of price reforms on domestic production are felt. In such cases, access to foreign exchange through the ESF program can be useful. In this view, a flexible aid program can help Egypt to adjust to temporary setbacks and facilitate the adoption of new policies, even if aid alone cannot do much to solve the underlying problems of the Egyptian economy.

Debt

Egypt enters the 1990s with a total indebtedness of about $50 billion. According to the World Bank, this places Egypt at the head of the list of heavily indebted countries when debt is measured as a percentage of gross domestic product (GDP).[47] Nearly $12 billion of the debt is owed to the United States, of which about half, some $6 billion, represents FMS credits extended in the fiscal 1979–84 period at a fixed weighted average interest rate of about 12 percent (see table A-2).[48]

Economic assistance loans have also totaled about $6 billion, though in most cases these are long-term loans at very concessional rates of interest.[49] Still, repayments on these loans add several hundred million dollars a year to Egypt's repayment burden.

During fiscal 1990 repayment to the United States on military loans, in the absence of another rescheduling agreement, will come to more than $700 million.[50] When nonmilitary loan repayments to the United States of nearly $350 million are

47. World Bank, Country Operations Division, *Arab Republic of Egypt: Country Economic Memorandum, Economic Readjustment with Growth*, vol. 1: *The Main Report*, Report 7447-EGT (Washington, D.C., January 5, 1989), pp. 89–97.

48. The original value of the FMS loans was $4.55 billion. Payments on these loans were deferred for two years from mid-1987 to mid-1989 as part of an overall rescheduling agreement with the Paris Club. These deferred payments are capitalized, that is, added to the outstanding balance, with the interest due based on prevailing market rates. Thus the total FMS debt as of mid-1988 stood at about $5.8 billion. By early 1990 the State Department was using $6.1 billion as the total of Egypt's FMS debt.

49. "Key Economic Indicators," in American Embassy, Cairo, "Egyptian Economic Trends," March 1989, p. 21.

50. The Department of Defense shows $720 million due in fiscal year 1990. See DOD, "Foreign Military Sales Credit Reporting System, Projection of Principal and Interest as of 9 November 1988, from 1 October 1988 to 30 September 2005," p. 93. According to these Defense Department figures, Egypt's repayment on the FMS debt, without rescheduling, will peak at over $1 billion a year in the mid-1990s.

added to the FMS payments, the total may slightly exceed the annual amount of economic assistance provided by the United States to Egypt in the same period.[51] In short, the Egyptian economy as a whole will be receiving no net inflow of capital from the United States to support economic development unless debt repayment is once again postponed.

Were Egypt unable or unwilling to make repayment on its debts to the United States (see table A-2), the Brooke Amendment to the Foreign Assistance Act would be triggered, which, as noted, requires the suspension of all aid to any country that falls behind by more than one year in debt repayment. A suspension of aid could, of course, be fatal to the U.S.-Egyptian relationship. Politicians on both sides will presumably ensure that such a drastic step is not taken. But the risk is there until some alternative is provided to help Egypt manage its debt repayments.

The Egyptian government has clearly been hoping that Washington will cancel or greatly reduce the outstanding debt. Washington has responded with various suggestions to reschedule or refinance some or all of the debt. Egyptians view rescheduling as simply pushing the problem off for a few years and making it even more difficult to manage at a later date.

Late in 1987 Congress passed legislation—the FY 1988 Foreign Operations Appropriations Bill—that would permit Egypt (and Israel) to refinance most of its high-interest debt on relatively attractive terms. Ninety percent of the debt would be covered by U.S. government guarantees, so private banks would assume little risk. Interest rates would be reduced to prevailing levels, but new repayment schedules would have to

51. In calendar year 1990 repayment of loans extended by the Agency for International Development, P.L. 480, the Commodity Credit Corporation, and the ExIm Bank will amount to $344 million unless there is a rescheduling agreement. All forms of grant economic aid to Egypt in 1990 will amount to about $1 billion. "Key Economic Indicators," p. 21.

be rigorously met. Israel eventually refinanced $4.7 billion of its FMS loans, thereby reducing its annual debt service payment by $150 million.[52] Egypt did not take up this option, perhaps fearing that refinancing would mean forgoing the chance of loan forgiveness. As a result, a cloud continues to hang over the U.S.-Egyptian relationship.[53]

52. Zuza, "Paper Examining Selected Options," p. 8.
53. During President Mubarak's April 1989 visit to Washington, economic issues loomed large in the discussions. Egypt was hoping for the early release of $230 million in cash assistance from fiscal years 1988 and 1989; the Bush administration was trying to use the release of the cash as a further incentive for Egypt to carry out economic reforms.

A Note on Economic Reform

No one contests the proposition that the Egyptian economy is in need of reform. The argument is over how, at what pace, and with what combination of pressure and inducements. This essay is not the place for an extensive treatment of Egypt's political economy.[54] But a few basic points need to be kept in mind.

Egypt is a fairly large country by world standards, having a population of more than 50 million and growing by nearly 1 million every nine months. It finds itself at the lower end of the middle-income countries, with a per capita income of about $700, depending on how the foreign exchange rate and the value of the informal economy are calculated.

Like many other developing countries, Egypt imports much more than it exports. According to American sources, imports in 1988–89 exceeded exports, including petroleum, by $8 billion.[55] To fill this hard-currency gap, Egypt relies on revenues from worker remittances, the Suez Canal, and tourism, which together bring in about $5 billion. Various donor contributions come to over $3.5 billion a year. These sums would place the hard-currency account in balance if it were not for the payments due on some $50 billion of debt. Even with concessional interest rates on much of this debt, repayment, barring rescheduling, will run at about $6 billion to $7 billion a year in the early 1990s (table A-3), well beyond Egypt's means.

54. For more extensive analysis, see Yahya Sadowski, *Political Vegetables? Businessman and Bureaucrat in the Reform of Egyptian Agriculture* (Brookings, forthcoming); John Waterbury, *The Egypt of Nasser and Sadat: The Political Economy of Two Regimes* (Princeton University Press, 1983); and Robert Springborg, *Mubarak's Egypt: Fragmentation of the Political Order* (Boulder, Colo.: Westview, 1989).

55. These and other figures in this section were provided by the American Embassy in Cairo in August 1989.

In 1987 it became clear that Egypt would no longer be able to make payments on its external debt. As mentioned, a standby agreement was negotiated with the IMF, which paved the way for Egypt to reschedule its debt repayments with its main creditors. But Egypt failed to follow through on the promised reforms. The standby agreement broke down. World Bank loans were not forthcoming, and by mid-1989 Egypt was obliged once again to make repayments on much of its debt.

Needless to say, Egypt made a renewed effort to reach a standby agreement with the IMF in order once again to reschedule debt repayments. In the early part of 1989 Egypt put together a plan for further reforms and budget reductions that the IMF was prepared to discuss. The IMF focused its attention on the size of the budget deficit, exchange rates, and interest rates, leaving to the World Bank the task of trying to persuade Egypt to make significant adjustments in its economy by removing subsidies on energy and some food products and by selling off some of the inefficient public sector enterprises.[56]

Assuming that the IMF does reach a standby agreement with Egypt in 1990, the door will again be open to debt rescheduling. But rescheduled debt is not forgiven debt. The payments that are postponed are simply added to the outstanding balance sheet of debt due, and prevailing rates of interest are charged on this recapitalized debt. In short, Egypt may buy time through the IMF–Paris Club measures, but there is always a next round to confront, at which point the debt issue looks even more formidable.

Economists have long debated whether Egypt can overcome

56. Even with proposed reforms, some prices will be held well below world market rates. For example, electricity sells for about one-fourth of the world market rate, thus encouraging a rapid increase in electricity and reducing the scope for larger oil exports. Bread prices, which have risen twice since 1985, are still one-fourth or so of the world price. But if bread prices were raised to world prices, and if consumption of bread did not decline, an average family would spend at least two-thirds of its income on bread. Fertilizer is also sold at about one-half the world price.

its economic problems and enter a period of sustained growth. Few would contest that bad policies have hampered growth in the past. But some of these policies are now deeply rooted and serve important political purposes. Any attempt to change them could be destabilizing. Egypt is also stuck with many problems in the short run that cannot be wished away. That the population is growing rapidly puts a tremendous burden on the government. Egypt's food import bill is huge and cannot easily be reduced soon. Egypt maintains a large and often inefficient bureaucracy. Finally, Egypt is at the mercy of the oil market, not so much because it exports oil, but because it derives secondary benefits from the oil market, primarily in the form of workers' remittances.

Admittedly, the picture has some bright spots. Tourist revenues have soared in recent years, particularly since the arrival of tourists from the oil-rich Arab countries. Egyptians hold a large quantity of foreign exchange in banks abroad, and in the right circumstances some of this money might be repatriated.[57] And Egypt has a lively informal economy that helps to augment the otherwise limited incomes of many Egyptians.[58]

Even if one comes to a fairly sanguine assessment of the Egyptian economy, Egypt will remain a poor, overly bureau-

57. Estimates run as high as $40 billion. Several factors work against repatriation of this capital. First, the Egyptian pound may be somewhat overvalued, so holders of dollars are reluctant to exchange at the official rate. Second, the exchange market is essentially one way. It is easy to change dollars to pounds at a fairly attractive rate, but it is not so easy to change pounds back into dollars. Therefore, those who may need dollars in the future tend to hold them. Third, interest rates on pound accounts in Egypt are less than the rate of inflation, whereas interest rates on dollar accounts are comparable to Eurobank rates. Fourth, there is still fear that the government may confiscate assets or investments in Egypt, as occurred in the 1960s. It may also take some time before wealthy Egyptians have confidence that the government will allow them to invest their money without a risk of nationalization.

58. See Delwin A. Roy, "The Hidden Economy in Egypt and Its Relationship to Current and Future Economic and Political Stability," January 1989.

cratized state for a long time. It will need large amounts of outside assistance. It will also need help with its debt problem, not only from the United States but also from its other major creditors.

Egyptians argue that they understand the need to reform the economy but that Egypt should not simply be dealt with "by the book." It needs time to introduce reforms, and it needs to take into account political reality. On the whole, the Egyptians have a good case to make. There is no point in trying to push too fast if the result might be political upheaval. Serious reform cannot simply be imposed from outside, or even by a few dedicated ministers. The Egyptians, especially at a time of political democratization, have to be given the chance to thrash out the political, economic, and social programs that suit them at this stage of their development. There are certain trade-offs between growth and equity, between efficiency and social justice, that no outsider should try to make for the Egyptians, since it is they who will have to live with the consequences of their policies. Egyptians have to be allowed to make their own mistakes.

This does not mean that the United States should just pour money into Egypt without asking any questions about how it will be used. But it does argue for a fairly relaxed and tolerant attitude as the Egyptians set their own agenda. It argues against the United States telling the Egyptians how to run their own economy. The IMF and World Bank can do so much more effectively, and the United States can make its views known within those institutions, but our own bilateral aid, especially military assistance, should be viewed primarily in the context of the political and strategic relationship that it was designed to support. If economic assistance can also be used to encourage reforms, fine, but that should be the third, not the first, priority.

U.S.-Egyptian Relations in the 1990s

Both Washington and Cairo need to think about how to restructure their bilateral relationship to serve their mutual interests in the 1990s, particularly in light of the dramatic changes taking place in the international arena. For the United States, this requires that we see Egypt as it is, not as we imagine it should be. The cold war prism is particularly inadequate for assessing U.S.-Egyptian relations in the decade ahead.

Nor should Egypt be viewed as another Israel, a country wedded to the United States by almost indissoluble bonds of interest and affection. The United States cannot realistically be expected to treat Egypt as it treats Israel, nor does Egypt want the same kind of intimate embrace. And yet officials in both Washington and Cairo often evoke the Israeli model as if it were applicable. Certainly the present U.S.-Egyptian relationship was forged in the course of the peace process and depends on continuing peace between Egypt and Israel. But Egypt is striving to regain a place of influence in the Arab world and will therefore be cautious in taking the lead in the peace process with Israel. With PLO support, Egypt can be an active participant in exploring procedural steps to start negotiations, but it will always be difficult for Egypt to depart from the broad Arab consensus on substantive issues of a peace settlement.

For the United States, the strategic value of Egypt resides in the fact that it is, on the whole, a force for stability in a volatile region, not that it is an ally in an anti-Soviet crusade. Egypt carries weight in inter-Arab circles, especially now that it has resumed relations with all major Arab capitals, including Damascus. From this perspective, the United States should be content to support Egypt as it plays its traditional role in the region, even though Egypt and the United States may sometimes find themselves on opposite sides of specific issues. Egypt may not become a model of economic efficiency, of export-led growth, of exemplary financial management, or of strategic cooperation. But Egypt is likely to remain at peace with its neighbors, including Israel, to muddle through in the face of daunting economic problems, so long as it continues to receive significant outside assistance, and to treat its own populace comparatively well. If, in addition, Egypt succeeds in democratizing, opening up its economy, normalizing relations with Israel, and promoting regional stability, so much the better. But even short of these lofty goals, Egypt deserves support.

So step one in restructuring the relationship means a shift toward realistic expectations. Egypt should be seen by Americans not solely as Israel's peace partner or as a strategic asset. Strategic cooperation may well be possible in individual cases, but that will not always be true and cannot be institutionalized in a formal alliance. Nor should the United States tie most of its economic support to reform on a liberal, capitalist model. In effect, expectations should be lowered, both in Washington and Cairo. Although they do share many interests, their interests are not identical, and the two countries are not destined to become full-fledged allies. That does not mean, however, that they should not aim for a continuing special relationship built on mutual interests.

Egypt stands to gain some and to lose some if this shift toward a more realistic basis for the relationship takes place. On the positive side, the quality of Egypt's relationship with Israel and its role in the peace process would not be the exclusive yardstick used to measure bilateral ties between Washington and Cairo, as has often seemed true in the past. Short of a return to active belligerency with Israel, Egypt would find itself freer to pursue what it perceives to be its own foreign policy interests without worrying excessively about the effect on U.S.

aid. In addition, Egypt would be under less American pressure to carry out joint operations against countries such as Libya. Nor would Egypt be urged to provide military bases for the United States. Major irritants would thereby be removed from the relationship.

On the negative side, Egypt could not expect to ride Israel's coattails as it has often done in the past. For example, if Israel received additional aid, Egypt could not always expect similar treatment (as happened in fiscal 1985, when both received substantial additions to their ESF accounts).[59] Nor would Egypt always be able to benefit from the same arrangements that Israel made to obtain advantageous terms for the purchase of military equipment, access to the most advanced technology, and so forth. In the future Egypt would not always be able to count on the privileges of being designated a non-NATO ally. But such privileges, in any case, have amounted to relatively little.[60]

A Proposal for Restructuring Aid and Debt

A more tangible loss to Egypt from the shift toward more realistic expectations on both sides of the relationship might be

59. Egyptians feel considerable ambivalence over whether they should be treated like Israel by the United States. On the one hand, the notion is widespread in Egypt that the Camp David Accords promised Egypt such equal treatment. On the other hand, Egyptians do not want to be seen as a full-fledged ally of the United States; they realize they cannot compete with Israel in the American political arena; and they see the growing disparity between the U.S.-Israeli relationship and their own ties with Washington. Still, many Egyptians would find the idea of a reduction of U.S. aid to Egypt more palatable if such action were paired with similar cuts to Israel. In domestic political terms, Mubarak would find it easier to explain across-the-board cuts to both Egypt and Israel than targeted reductions in American aid to Egypt.

60. For example, both Israel and Egypt have been eligible to bid on contracts for various aspects of the strategic defense initiative. Israel, with its advantage in electronics and sophisticated military technology, has been able to make good use of this provision; Egypt has been much less successful.

a decrease in aid. Congress may be unwilling to continue to support Egypt at such high levels, especially if the justification is no longer couched in terms of a strategic alliance against the Soviet Union or investment in further steps in the peace process. But such a drop in aid levels, even for Egypt and Israel, may well be in the offing in any event as part of an overall reassessment of the aid program worldwide.[61]

In theory, Egypt could get more real benefit from a smaller but better structured aid program. The key to such a revised program would be significant debt relief. Most analysts now agree that heavily indebted countries, such as Egypt, cannot grow out of their economic problems simply by borrowing more money and making needed economic reforms. The Brady Plan, put forward by President Bush's secretary of the treasury, Nicholas F. Brady, envisages a multilateral program to encourage private banks to write off part of their loans to developing countries in exchange for guarantees of repayment of the remainder of the outstanding debt. It makes no provision for countries like Egypt, however, that have borrowed almost entirely from governments, not private banks.

The most onerous of Egypt's debts to the United States are the FMS credits that were extended from fiscal years 1979 to 1984. These were contracted at high rates of interest, averaging nearly 12 percent. Without continued rescheduling agreements, repayment of these loans will cost Egypt some $850 million a year through the mid-1990s.[62] With rescheduling, Egypt could buy time, but the ultimate size of the debt burden will simply continue to grow as postponed payments are recapitalized and added to the stock of outstanding debt.

61. See, for example, the following critical evaluations of U.S. foreign assistance: Administrator, U.S. Agency for International Development, *Development and the National Interest: U.S. Economic Assistance into the 21st Century* (1989); and *Report of the Task Force on Foreign Assistance*, Committee Print, House Committee on Foreign Affairs, 101 Cong. 1 sess. (GPO, February 1989).

62. Derived from DOD, "Foreign Military Sales Credit Reporting System."

The United States should consider offering the Egyptians the following trade-off: all or part of the FMS debt would be written off in return for an Egyptian agreement to a reduction of FMS grant aid from the current level of $1.3 billion. Washington should make it clear that as part of any debt-relief proposal, Congress would expect continued evidence that Egypt is tackling its economic problems through serious reform efforts, but rigid reform criteria should be avoided. The primary link should be between reducing the debt and cutting back on the FMS program. Economic reform would become a secondary concern for the U.S. government, although the IMF and World Bank would continue to use their influence to push Egypt in that direction.[63] The goal for the United States would be to contribute to Egypt's economic health by substantially reducing its outstanding indebtedness by the end of the 1990s. Reduction of debt owed to the United States could help to break the vicious cycle of Egyptian dependence, which will otherwise risk triggering default and suspension of all U.S. aid. It could also help to persuade other creditors to take similar steps, which might leave Egypt with manageable debt service obligations by the mid-1990s.

The cleanest approach would be a one-time congressional act to waive repayment of the entire FMS debt, which would have an immediate beneficial effect on the Egyptian economy. By simultaneously reducing new FMS outlays by most of the amount Egypt would otherwise be repaying on past FMS debt, new FMS obligations would come to about $800 million annually. Assuming that Egypt would otherwise continue to receive FMS aid at levels prevailing since 1983—about $1.3 billion yearly—this reduced level of funding would mean that the

63. The United States cannot entirely hide behind the IMF and World Bank as these institutions pressure Egypt to reform its economy. Nonetheless, the multilateral nature of these institutions helps to keep arguments over reform from becoming major problems in the U.S.-Egyptian relationship.

equivalent of the forgiven FMS foreign debt would have been "saved" by the year 2000.[64]

Alternatively, a more gradual transition could be made, writing off smaller amounts of the debt and reducing FMS more slowly. But the principle to be followed here, it would seem, should be to go to Congress as few times as possible on this issue.

It will be argued, especially by some Egyptian officials, that any reduction in the FMS program would signal a weakening of American support for Egypt. The Egyptian military might respond by criticizing the regime for mismanaging the relationship with the United States.

These are arguments that need to be carefully considered, but they should not go unchallenged. First, there is no reason to equate levels of FMS to levels of support for Egypt. After all, the point of reducing both debt and FMS aid is to provide more real aid to the Egyptian economy, not less. Second, Egyptian military purchases from the United States need not be exclu-

64. This approach to debt relief—known within the bureaucracy as the buy-out option—would freeze the current FMS debt at its nearly $6 billion level and would then proceed to pay off the entire debt over an eight- to ten-year period with funds that otherwise would have gone to Egypt as new aid. There is no actual need for the process to take such a form, since Congress has the authority to cancel outstanding debt, but such an action would create a precedent that few in Congress would favor. Therefore, and to win congressional support, the administration may have to point to FMS reductions (and perhaps some ESF reductions as well) of a significant amount over a period of years to account for how the FMS debt is to be "bought out" without creating unwelcome precedents. This problem is particularly acute because the FMS credits were provided through the Federal Financing Bank, which also provides credits to American farmers and small businessmen. Any write-off of Egyptian FMS debt would risk serving as a precedent for these powerful domestic constituencies. Thus Congress has a political need to demonstrate that the debt is not simply being canceled, but rather that it is being paid off by funds that would otherwise be going to Egypt to purchase more arms. The cost of this option to the U.S. taxpayer amounts to the interest on the FMS debt that would be forgone once the debt was "capped" or paid off.

sively determined by the FMS program. Egypt could use some of the foreign exchange that would otherwise be spent on debt repayment to purchase arms, if indeed that is seen as a high national priority. Moreover, Egypt may be able to raise funds from some of the oil-rich Gulf states in order to purchase arms, thereby reviving an earlier framework for Arab military and industrial cooperation. Third, Egypt should, in any case, be asking itself how large a military establishment it needs at a time of relative regional stability. Nowhere is Egypt exposed to a large external threat. Were any such threat to develop, the United States might well be asked to increase its support. In short, Egypt needs to think about military expenditures, including the FMS program, as it tries to reform its economy and reduce its budget deficit. Certainly the United States and the Soviet Union have come to recognize that economic progress requires careful regulation of military spending; the same should be true for Egypt. Finally, Egypt is likely to face the prospect at some point of reduced aid, and it would be better off trying to negotiate a package of debt reduction combined with reduced aid than simply to see aid dwindle because of "donor fatigue" in Washington and competing demands from other aid claimants, including countries in central Europe.

As for economic assistance, the United States should consider offering Egypt a similar package of less but "better" aid. Egypt wants a maximum of cash transfer and a minimum of strings. Economic aid of all kinds now totals nearly $1 billion, but much of it is tied to projects, importation of specific commodities, or concessional wheat sales. Only $115 million is provided in the form of cash, and that is only released when certain economic reforms have been taken.

A smaller program of about $750 million might be phased in over several years that would give Egypt more flexibility in deciding how to use the aid. Its core components would be a cash transfer (balance-of-payments support) of $500 million; $150 million in projects, with emphasis on small, Egyptian-designed initiatives; and an option of $150 million worth of P.L. 480 purchases (mostly wheat and flour) or $100 million in cash.[65] For the American taxpayer, the last element of cash transfer or P.L. 480 aid is nearly equivalent if one assumes that 60 percent of the P.L. 480 program is in the form of grants.[66]

This proposal would eliminate entirely the commodity import program, which has represented about one-third of the economic support fund. It has been justified in the past because it is a "quick dispersing" form of aid. That is to say, Egypt can immediately use concessional credits to buy commodities on the American market. American producers are fond of the program because it involves a government subsidy—easy credits—to help sell their goods abroad. The Egyptians accept the commodity import program because it is available, but they would much rather receive a straight cash transfer. The program has the disadvantage of forcing the Egyptians to buy American goods at prices that may be comparatively high simply because the subsidized credits are available. This pressure can have a distorting effect on the Egyptian economy and may in some cases undercut the strength of local markets. If the program is retained, it should be carefully regulated to make sure that it is actually benefiting Egypt.

To summarize, a revised package of American aid to Egypt for the mid-1990s might well take the following form:

---

65. Egypt could continue to receive commodity export credit guarantees, as it does now, but these short-term credits are not highly concessional and should not be equated with the aid program, most of which is in the form of grants or very soft loans.

66. Richard N. Blue and others, *PL 480 Title I: The Egyptian Case*, A.I.D. Project Impact Evaluation Report 45 (U.S. Agency for International Development, June 1983).

Component	Amount (1990 dollars)
Foreign military sales grants	800 million
Economic support fund cash grants	500 million
Project aid	150 million
Public Law 480	150 million
(Alternative to P.L. 480)	(100 million additional cash transfer)

Assuming that FMS debt repayments had been canceled as part of this package (saving Egypt some $850 million a year during the 1990s), and that repayments on other outstanding debt to the United States would run about $200 million a year, this revised program would mean a net inflow of new aid to Egypt of about $1.4 billion (in 1990 dollars). This figure is comparable to the net inflow of about $1.3 billion in the current American aid program (assuming debt repayment is being made).

In brief, a smaller program, with proper restructuring, combined with writing off the FMS loan repayments, would actually be more beneficial for Egypt and would be no more costly to the American taxpayer through the 1990s. Egypt not only would be receiving somewhat more net assistance but would also have much more flexibility in deciding how to use the aid. In addition, both countries would benefit from a reduction in the size of the AID mission in Egypt.

As the table above shows, once the transition to a revised aid package has been made, Egypt will receive a larger proportion of American assistance in the useful form of untied foreign exchange. Nothing will prevent Egypt from deciding to use its foreign currency to purchase arms or wheat, from the United States or elsewhere, but the decisions will be Egypt's to make. In any event, Egypt will have been relieved of a significant part of its debt burden and will have more discretion in how it chooses to use its remaining aid. What may be lost is some degree of American leverage to urge the Egyptians to continue to reform their economy. Some of that pressure, however, will continue because of IMF recommendations and Paris Club requirements for rescheduling other outstanding debt.[67] This proposal does not, after all, call for the United States to write off all its government-to-government debt.

By writing off only FMS debt, the United States will not set a precedent for all other debt, since it can be argued that FMS credits to buy arms do nothing to enhance the productive sectors of the economy, unlike development loans for projects, which can ultimately pay for themselves. (The decision in fiscal 1985 to put all FMS aid to Egypt and Israel on a grant basis was a belated recognition of this fact.) The United States would also be recognizing that its own security interests are served by providing American arms to Egypt.

Some Egyptians may believe that pressures are building to write off much of their foreign debt. The countries of the European Community have already shown a willingness to write off debts incurred by sub-Saharan African countries. The Brady Plan was the basis for reducing Mexico's debt payment burden by about 10 percent, and other countries may follow suit.[68]

Obviously, if Egypt has the option of keeping the current aid program intact at present levels, while at the same time having

67. For arguments in favor of maintaining a link between debt relief and economic reform, see Delwin A. Roy, "Egyptian Debt: Forgive—or Forget?" 1989, especially pp. 21–25.

68. The experience of Mexico with the Brady Plan, however, is not particularly encouraging for Egypt. After adopting most of the reforms required by the IMF, and after lengthy negotiations, Mexico in July 1989 reached an agreement with creditors that was likely to improve its annual cash flow by $1.7 billion to $2.0 billion through a combination of debt reduction, reduced interest rates, and new loans. See Edward R. Fried and Philip H. Trezise, "Third World Debt: Phase Three Begins," *Brookings Review*, vol. 7 (Fall 1989), pp. 29–31. The final agreement, signed in February 1990, is analyzed by Nora Lustig, "Agreement Signed by Mexico and Its Commercial Banks," testimony before the Subcommittee on International Development, Finance, Trade and Monetary Policy of the House Committee on Banking, Finance and Urban Affairs, February 7, 1990.

its debt to the United States greatly reduced, then it would prefer that option. But there are no signs that Congress is in a mood for such dramatic action on debt reduction for Egypt or for anyone else. The suggestion made here of tying debt reduction to a smaller overall aid program in Egypt is designed to overcome congressional reticence.

Let us assume that the United States sets itself a target of restructuring its aid relationship with Egypt, along the lines mentioned, by fiscal 1995. This would give enough time to arrange a smooth transition with the government of Egypt, to build congressional support, and to work with other creditors in the Paris Club to try to multilateralize debt-relief arrangements. Since most of Egypt's debt is to countries other than the United States, it will be important to try to persuade them to follow the American lead. But if Washington balks, others probably will as well, leaving Egypt in constant danger of default.

Why should Congress go along with such a plan of debt relief? First, cutting aid to Egypt to about $1.6 billion a year by the mid-1990s would mean a savings of several billion dollars (in current dollars) from the FMS and ESF accounts between now and then. These funds could conceivably be reprogrammed for other purposes.

Second, although writing off the FMS debt will cost the American Treasury something in theory, the reality may be quite different. It seems unlikely that this debt will be entirely repaid, but even if it is, new cash outlays from Washington will probably be needed to service the debt well into the future.[69] If this assumption is valid, the United States will suffer no real loss. Even if the assumption is wrong, the reduction in the total level of aid will in time make up for losses incurred in the can-

69. In making its budget projections for the future, neither the Office of Management and Budget nor the Congressional Budget Office assumes that Egypt will make any repayments on its outstanding debt.

celing of the FMS debt.[70] Indeed, by the second half of the 1990s at the latest, the issue of FMS debt should be fully resolved, relieving Egypt and the U.S.-Egyptian relationship of an otherwise unmanageable burden.[71] Reducing FMS outlays to Egypt (and Israel?) would also appeal to those in Congress who would like to see the arms buildup in the region slow down. In a post–cold war atmosphere it makes less and less sense to provide large amounts of arms for strategic reasons, although regional considerations will still have to be taken into account.

Why would the Egyptians favor this approach of less but better aid? First, it holds out the promise of removing the biggest problem in the bilateral relationship, the repayment of military debt. As long as this issue confronts Egypt, there will always be the possibility of default, which would then entail the suspension of all U.S. aid. Second, Egypt would have much more flexibility in using the aid provided. Most important for Egypt, the bulk of the aid would be available as cash transfer. Admittedly, Congress might react negatively to such a large cash transfer component of the aid program. Evidence of misuse of funds, blatant cases of corruption, or the perception that Egypt is not serious about reforming its economy could reduce congressional support for the program. But these risks accompany any program, including the present one, and to date the U.S. aid program in Egypt has been free of large-scale corruption.

In assessing the proposed alternative, Egyptians and Americans should think of the costs of continuing with incremental

70. The legal difficulties entailed in restructuring FMS loans are spelled out in detail in a letter to Representative David R. Obey from the Comptroller General of the United States on July 21, 1987.

71. A reduction in the Egyptian program might also open the way for a restructuring and reduction of the huge aid program to Israel, where today most new economic assistance simply goes to paying off old loans.

adjustments in the current program. The present system allows Egypt to muddle through, but the United States inevitably finds itself in the position of pressuring Egypt for reforms, then relenting at the last moment in the face of the consequences of default. The two countries then do enough to meet legal deadlines, to avoid a total breach, and to push the problem down the road for a while. At best, they buy time. Optimists profess that the time thus gained can be used to reform the economy, enhance productivity, and so forth—all worthy goals—and that the ultimate debt problem will seem less daunting once the Egyptian economy is functioning at its full capacity.

Others, less optimistic, see Egypt trapped in a vicious circle caused by heavy indebtedness, politically motivated subsidies, and dependence on uncertain oil revenues and petrodollars, as well as shackled with a centralized political system in which ministers constantly pass the buck to the president, who then tries to find political solutions to economic problems. In such a system, those who hold the whip—whether the IMF or the United States or the oil-rich Arabs—cannot expect to win much gratitude, even when their advice may be well-meaning and to the point.

Thus if one accepts that the underlying rationale for the U.S.-Egyptian relationship is political and strategic, those should be the primary criteria used in addressing the economic side of the relationship. To protect the quality of the relationship between Cairo and Washington, the two countries must get beyond arguments over aid and debt. To preserve the Egyptian-Israeli peace and Egypt's role as a force for moderation in the broader Arab world, the United States must be careful not to press Egypt to the point where the regime's stability and legitimacy are jeopardized. Both sets of objectives would be well served by taking a bold approach to resolving the debt and aid problems. The alternative incrementalist approach is a guarantee of continued friction, a source of ill will, and a formula for long-term damage to the relationship.

Reviving the Peace Process

Debt relief and a restructured aid program are both tangible steps that the United States can take to strengthen the underpinnings of the U.S.-Egyptian relationship. Just as important, however, is the less tangible issue of reviving the Arab-Israeli peace process. Few observers would disagree with the view that a sharp deterioration of the general Arab-Israeli situation, such as a Syrian-Israeli war or a marked escalation of violence in the Israeli-occupied territories, would not go unnoticed in Cairo.

Now that Egypt is back in the Arab League and has restored relations with all Arab countries, Cairo can be expected to support the mainstream Palestinian position quite faithfully, while working hard to bring Palestinians into negotiations with Israel. Both U.S.-Egyptian and Egyptian-Israeli relations therefore depend to some degree on how the peace process unfolds.

Since the beginning of the Palestinian *intifadah* in December 1987, Egypt has been trying to encourage the start of an Israeli-PLO dialogue as a first step toward convening an international conference on the Middle East. The beginning of the U.S.-PLO dialogue in December 1988 was welcomed in Cairo, and considerable parallel American and Egyptian diplomatic effort has subsequently taken place. But all these initiatives may founder on the rock of Prime Minister Shamir's adamant refusal to deal with the PLO.

In theory, several ways out of the impasse exist. It may be possible to start negotiations between Israelis and non-PLO Palestinians. That is Shamir's preference. Or it may be necessary to wait until Shamir and the Likud bloc are replaced by a more flexible Israeli leadership. Or it may be feasible for the PLO to moderate its positions to the point where even Shamir and his Likud colleagues agree to deal with it, at least indirectly.

Whatever their preferences may be, Washington, Cairo, and

the PLO will all probably have to deal with an Israeli government that adopts a hard line on accepting the PLO, on relinquishing occupied territory, and on respecting Palestinian national rights. And whatever the Israelis and some Americans may hope, no Palestinians are likely to agree to negotiate with Israel, nor would they have much authority if they were to do so, unless the PLO gives its stamp of approval. How then might the circle be squared, or must we resign ourselves to the prospect of a prolonged stalemate, with all the dangers of growing extremism and violence that might follow from the collapse of the peace process?

The Bush administration made it clear from the beginning that it would not put forward a peace plan of its own, but it did strongly encourage Prime Minister Shamir to do so. The result came in the form of a general Israeli proposal in May 1989 that adhered quite closely to past positions, including the Camp David Accords, with the added innovation of calling for elections in the West Bank and Gaza to select a Palestinian negotiating team with which Israel would discuss the arrangements for a transitional period, as called for in Camp David.[72]

The Israeli proposal left many questions unanswered—for example, the participation of Palestinians residing in East Jerusalem as candidates and electors—but it was the kind of proposal that attracts sympathetic attention in Washington. Optimists saw it as a way for Shamir to begin talks with Palestinians, who would no doubt be PLO supporters, but to do so through a mechanism—elections—that would give legitimacy to the process in the eyes of most Israelis. Pessimists, in contrast, saw the proposal as a gimmick for Shamir to ward off American pressures; to put the ball in the Palestinian court, where it might well stay for some time; to drive a wedge be-

---

72. The text of the Shamir plan can be found in "A Peace Initiative—Document," *Jerusalem Post*, May 15, 1989, p. 2, in FBIS, *NESA*, May 15, 1989, pp. 28–30.

tween the Palestinians under occupation and those outside; and to bring the *intifadah* to an end.

The Egyptians initially viewed the election proposal with considerable skepticism as did most other Arabs, including the PLO. Egypt was particularly eager not to get too far out of touch with mainstream Arab sentiment, since the Arab League was on the verge of readmitting Egypt. At the same time Egypt's genuine concern for promoting the peace process, plus its desire to remain on good terms with Washington, required Egypt to adopt a moderate stance toward the Shamir proposal, raising questions and seeking clarifications but, above all, not rejecting it.

It soon became clear that the PLO also did not want to be in the position of rejecting the Shamir plan in its entirety, since that might damage the U.S.-PLO dialogue and could leave the impression that the PLO was refusing a plausible approach to peacemaking. Instead of saying no, the PLO began to develop conditions of its own for holding elections. They would have to be genuinely free and be held under international supervision, with the full participation of the Palestinians living in East Jerusalem, and with a prior commitment from Israel to the principle of "land for peace," as called for in UN Resolution 242.[73] All these points were conveyed to Israel by the Egyptians in July 1989 as well as by Soviet and American intermediaries.[74]

Unfortunately for the peace process, the PLO's conditions conflicted with conditions set by the Likud party that same month. The party forced Shamir to agree to the following

73. Palestinian sources also spoke in the summer of 1989 of the possibility that Egyptians and Americans might be asked to observe any elections in the West Bank and Gaza to ensure their fairness.

74. Egypt eventually formalized these positions in a ten-point plan that was variously described as an alternative to Shamir's plan or a clarification of it. See Joel Brinkley, "Israel Is Sending Rabin to Cairo on Voting Plan," *New York Times*, September 18, 1989, pp. A1, A8, for background on the Egyptian plan.

points: the Palestinians in East Jerusalem would not be allowed to participate in the voting; settlements in the occupied territory would continue to be built; Israel would not agree to withdraw from the occupied territories and would not permit the establishment of a Palestinian state; and no elections would take place until the uprising ended.[75]

At this point the United States and Egypt began to coordinate their efforts, and Cairo took upon itself the role of communicating between Washington and the PLO leader, Yasir Arafat. This arrangement had several advantages. Egypt could not only talk directly with Arafat and other high-ranking PLO officials (something the United States still refused to do) but could also front for the PLO. In effect, Egypt could help Israeli Prime Minister Shamir preserve the fiction that the PLO was not directly involved in this initial round of diplomatic jousting. Egypt might consult with the PLO, but it was with Egypt that both the United States and Israel would be dealing. With such diplomatic niceties it is sometimes possible to overcome otherwise intractable obstacles. That, at least, was the American hope.

The fall of 1989 was filled with a series of points and counterpoints passed among the parties. Shamir's four points were responded to with an Egyptian ten-point plan, which seemed to reflect PLO views.[76] Somewhat reluctantly, U.S. Secretary of State James Baker joined the game in October 1989 with a five-point plan of his own.[77]

Baker's plan called for trilateral U.S.-Israeli-Egyptian talks at

75. See Joel Brinkley, "Shamir Accepts Hard-Line Moves That Imperil Arab Elections Plan," *New York Times*, July 6, 1989, pp. A1, A10.

76. See *Jerusalem Post* (International Edition), September 23, 1989, p. 2, for a summary of the Egyptian ten-point proposal.

77. The final text of the "Baker Plan," as released by the State Department, can be found in Thomas L. Friedman, "Advance Reported on Mideast Talks," *New York Times*, December 7, 1989, p. A11. Earlier versions appeared in Menachem Shalev, "Official Version of 'Five Points,'" *Jerusalem Post*, October 17, 1989.

the foreign minister level to sort out the procedural arrangements for holding Israeli-Palestinian talks in Cairo to discuss elections. Israel hesitantly gave its agreement on November 5, 1989, but spelled out several "assumptions" that seemed to condition the acceptance. After considerable diplomatic maneuvering, Egypt conveyed a message to Washington on December 6, 1989, that Baker chose to interpret as acceptance of his five-point proposal. Whatever conditions or assumptions were attached were conveniently ignored.

In brief, the stage was set by early 1990 for a symbolically important, but substantively limited, step in reviving the peace process. Egypt (with little opposition from any Arab party) would host a meeting of Israelis and Palestinians to discuss elections in the West Bank and Gaza and other pertinent issues. Whatever the fate of this exercise, it has already demonstrated that the United States and Egypt can work closely together in the peace process, and that Egypt has the ability not only to reflect the PLO view but also to help support moderate tendencies within the Palestinian movement.[78]

Beyond the issue of elections in the West Bank and Gaza, of course, lie the larger issues of a comprehensive Arab-Israeli peace. Egypt will find it difficult to continue playing a helpful role when such substantive issues as borders, Jerusalem, and Palestinian rights are placed on the agenda. For domestic and regional reasons, Egypt cannot mediate between Israel and the Palestinians on these matters. But if Egypt, working closely

78. The two most difficult issues dividing the Israelis and Palestinians were the composition of the Palestinian negotiating team and the agenda. Israel wanted to limit Palestinian participation in the talks to inhabitants of "Judea and Samaria." Some in the Likud would even exclude Palestinians residing in East Jerusalem. The PLO insisted on the participation of "insiders" and "outsiders," although it was understood that Israel would refuse to sit with any Palestinians who were actual members of the PLO leadership. Concerning the agenda, Israel insisted on discussing only its election plan. The PLO agreed to discuss elections "and other issues" relating to the negotiations.

with the United States, can help bring about serious Israeli-Palestinian negotiations, it will have made an important contribution to peace. It will also have strengthened one of the important strands of the U.S.-Egyptian relationship. For those in Congress who ask what the United States gets for its aid to Egypt, the answer may again be, "help in achieving an Arab-Israeli peace settlement."

Conclusion

As Washington and Cairo look forward to their relationship in the 1990s, both have cause for satisfaction as well as concern. On the positive side, the Egyptian-Israeli peace has endured and has not proved to be an obstacle to Egypt's return to a position of influence in the Arab world. Although some Arabs still criticize Egypt for having made a separate peace with Israel, the PLO is actively cooperating with both Egypt and the United States to try to revive the peace process, and the Arab League has gone on record in support of this strategy.[79] For the moment a full-scale Arab-Israeli war seems remote, and Egypt's being at peace with Israel is one of the reasons.

Egypt's strategic importance in promoting stability in the Middle East and ensuring the absence of a credible Arab military option against Israel is precisely the reason behind American willingness to provide Egypt with large amounts of aid. No other third world country has been treated more generously by the U.S. Congress. And for the moment there are few signs that Congress wants to stop giving that assistance.

Egypt has reason to be satisfied that it has recovered its national territory, has enjoyed more than fifteen years of peace, and has been able to reestablish normal relations with most Arab countries. The same cannot be said about the "prosperity" part of the "peace and prosperity" promise that President Anwar Sadat held out to his people when he took Egypt into the American camp. Only when oil prices have been on the

79. At the Arab summit held in Casablanca in May 1989, the members of the Arab League endorsed the new position of the PLO, including its acceptance of UN Resolutions 242 and 338 and its call for a two-state settlement of the Palestinian question.

rise has the Egyptian economy seemed to flourish, and oil prices are beyond Egypt's control.

Since 1985 Egypt's economic reality has been generally discouraging. Foreign exchange earnings have been inadequate to finance imports and have led to the accumulation of a large external debt. Like many other countries, Egypt spends more than it takes in, leaving large budget deficits. Inflation has become a persistent problem. Price reform has taken place, but slowly and always with an eye toward the political consequences of lifting subsidies on food and energy prices too quickly. The International Monetary Fund has prescribed many belt-tightening measures, and the United States has lent its weight to these efforts to encourage reform. If reform is indeed the answer to Egypt's problems, the results lie somewhere in the future; the present situation seems far from either the hoped-for prosperity or a breakthrough to self-sustaining growth. Economic issues have now become a critical issue in the U.S.-Egyptian relationship, and they could well become even more difficult without serious steps to deal with debt and to restructure the aid program.

The United States has clearly benefited from a decade of good relations with Egypt. In many ways this relationship represents a rare success story for the United States in a region where such successes have been few and far between.[80] As is often true, however, success may breed a sort of complacency, a feeling that all is well, that no new decisions are needed. Such attitudes could be detrimental to U.S.-Egyptian relations in the 1990s. Cairo should not be taken for granted.

As discussed earlier, Washington must deal with two large

80. It is worth underscoring that the United States has been represented in Cairo since 1974 by superb American ambassadors drawn from the top ranks of the foreign service. The American ambassador in Cairo plays a crucial role in the relationship, and it is therefore of great importance whom President Bush sends in 1991 to replace Frank G. Wisner, who has enjoyed an unusually good reputation among Egyptians of diverse backgrounds.

issues if relations with Cairo are to be kept on a steady basis. One set of decisions—on debt relief and the restructuring of the aid program—is entirely within the power of the United States to act upon. This does not mean these decisions will be easy to carry out, for there will be opposition from within the bureaucracy and from Congress. Strong presidential leadership will be needed, and that may require some "peg" on which to hang a new policy. For example, if Egypt is especially helpful in the peace process, the president may find it easier than it otherwise might be to ask Congress to tackle the debt and aid problems. But even without such a development on the peace front, Egypt's economic problems need attention from Washington. The answer does not lie in new obligations alone; it also means debt reduction and an improved aid package.

In the final analysis, however, the United States cannot buy good relations with Egypt. These will always depend in large part on developments elsewhere in the Middle East region. Egypt cannot stand entirely apart from a Middle East caught up in wars and political extremism. Most of the currents that are affecting the Middle East are beyond Washington's control. That is certainly true of Islamic extremism. But it is not entirely true of the Arab-Israeli peace process.

Admittedly, the United States faces severe constraints in using its influence to promote Israeli-Palestinian reconciliation, but it is simply wrong to say that the United States can do nothing at all. Indeed, for the sake of its broad interests in the region it must remain active in promoting a broadening of the peace process. Not only can this help to prevent the growth of extremism in both Israel and some Arab circles, but it can also help to reinforce the peace that already exists between Egypt and Israel. Not incidentally, the United States would also be strengthening its relations with Cairo and thereby helping to preserve into the 1990s a relationship that has served its interests well.

TABLE A-1. U.S. ECONOMIC AND MILITARY ASSISTANCE TO EGYPT SINCE CAMP DAVID, FISCAL YEARS 1979–90, AND TOTALS FROM 1974–90

Millions of current dollars

Item	1979	1980	1981	1982	1983	1984	1985	1986	1987	1988	1989	1990[a]	Aid totals	
													1974–90	1981–90
Foreign military sales	0	0	550	900	1,325	1,365	1,175	1,244	1,300	1,300	1,300	1,294	11,754	11,754
Forgiven credits (grants)	...	...	...	200	425	465	1,175	1,244	1,300	1,300	1,300	1,294	8,704	8,704
Guaranteed credits	...	...	550	700	900	900	...	...	...	...	...	...	3,050	3,050
Camp David military aid loan (FMS credit)	1,500	...	...	...	...	...	...	...	...	...	...	...	1,500	...
International military education and training	0	1	1	2	2	2	2	2	2	2	2	2	20	19
Economic support fund	835	865	829	771	750	750	1,315	780	815	815	815	812	12,655	8,452
Grant	585	585	759	771	750	750	1,315	780	815	815	815	812	10,000	8,382
Loan	250	280	70	...	...	...	...	...	...	...	...	...	2,655	70
Public Law 480														
Title I	253	301	301	294	262	269	238	222	182	181	172	160	3,458	2,281
Title II	231	285	273	262	250	250	225	213	178	180	170	160	3,269	2,161
Export-Import Bank financing	22	16	29	32	12	19	13	9	4	1	2	...	189	121
Direct loans	109	96	65	67	76	206	48	39	3	0	0	0	835	504
Guarantees	91	10	17	42	8	156	0	0	0	0	0	0	400	223
Insurance	12	50	32	23	61	48	45	34	2	...	...	...	357	244
USIA Exchanges	5	36	15	3	7	2	3	5	1	...	...	...	78	36
American schools and hospitals abroad	1	1	1	1	1	1	1	1	1	1	1	n.a.	11	8
Total	2,698	1,264	1,747	2,036	2,416	2,594	2,782	2,291	2,304	2,301	2,290	2,268	30,243	23,027

SOURCE: Office of Management and Budget, "U.S. Foreign Assistance Program to Egypt," February 1990. Figures may not add because of rounding.
n.a. Not available.
a. Estimated.

TABLE A-2. EGYPTIAN DEBT TO THE U.S. GOVERNMENT, CALENDAR YEARS 1989, 1990

Millions of current dollars

Item	Outstanding (as of June 30, 1988)	Payments due during	
		1989	1990
Total	11,731	952	948
U.S. Agency for International Development	2,605	103	112
Foreign military sales	5,775	574	604
Public Law 480	2,632	81	100
Commodity Credit Corporation	522	164	107
Export-Import Bank	197	30	25

SOURCE: "Key Economic Indicators," in American Embassy, Cairo, "Egyptian Economic Trends," March 1989, p. 21.

TABLE A-3. EGYPT'S DEBT SERVICE, FISCAL YEARS 1985–92

Millions of current dollars

Year	Civilian	Civilian, plus estimated military	Civilian, estimated military, plus interest on short-term debt
1985	3,053	4,200	4,789
1986	3,580	4,813	5,229
1987	4,071	5,775	6,062
1988 (after rescheduling)[a]	1,138	1,138	1,436
1989 (without rescheduling)[a]	4,954	6,303	6,613
1990[a]	5,468	6,818	7,141
1991[a]	5,121	6,513	6,849
1992[a]	6,180	7,681	8,030

SOURCE: World Bank, Country Operations Division, *Egypt: Country Economic Memorandum, Economic Readjustment with Growth,* vol. 2: *Annexes,* Report 7447-EGT (Washington, D.C., January 5, 1989), p. 23, table 4.9.
   a. Estimated.

Index

11.80